SIMPLE SONGS FOR BASS

THE EASIEST BASS GUITAR SONGBOOK EVER

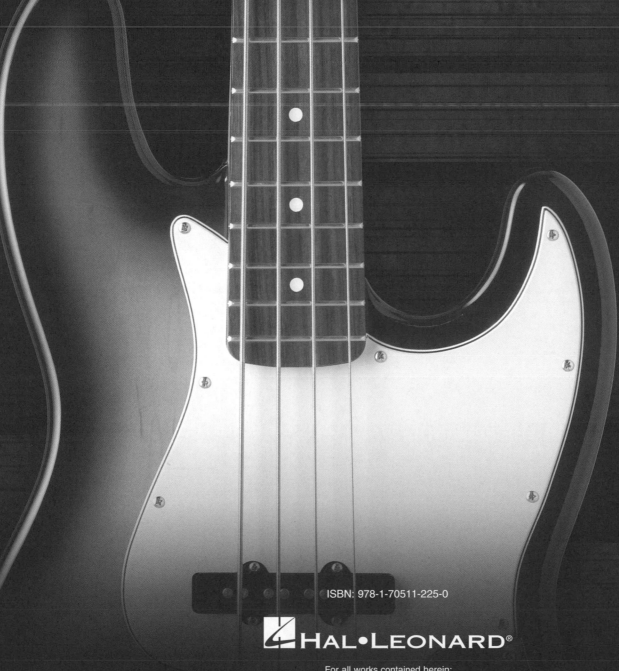

ISBN: 978-1-70511-225-0

HAL•LEONARD®

Visit Hal Leonard Online at
www.halleonard.com

Contact us:
Hal Leonard
7777 West Bluemound Road
Milwaukee, WI 53213
Email: info@halleonard.com

In Europe, contact:
Hal Leonard Europe Limited
42 Wigmore Street
Marylebone, London, W1U 2RN
Email: info@halleonardeurope.com

In Australia, contact:
Hal Leonard Australia Pty. Ltd.
4 Lentara Court
Cheltenham, Victoria, 3192 Australia
Email: info@halleonard.com.au

Bass Rhythm Tab Legend

Rhythm Tab is a form of notation that adds rhythmic values to the traditional tab staff.

TABLATURE graphically represents the bass guitar fingerboard. Each horizontal line represents a string, and each number represents a fret. Rhythmic values are shown using ovals, stems, and dots.

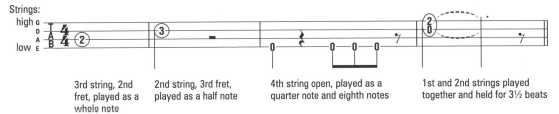

Strings: high G D A low E

3rd string, 2nd fret, played as a whole note

2nd string, 3rd fret, played as a half note

4th string open, played as a quarter note and eighth notes

1st and 2nd strings played together and held for 3½ beats

Definitions for Special Notation

QUARTER-STEP BEND: Strike the note and bend up 1/4 step.

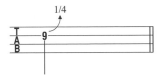

BEND AND RELEASE: Strike the note and bend up as indicated, then release back to the original note. Only the first note is struck.

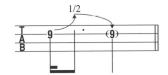

VIBRATO: The string is vibrated by rapidly bending and releasing the note with the fretting hand.

HAMMER-ON: Strike the first (lower) note with one finger, then sound the higher note (on the same string) with another finger by fretting it without picking

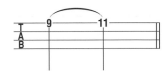

PULL-OFF: Place both fingers on the notes to be sounded. Strike the first note, and without picking, pull the finger off to sound the second (lower) note.

LEGATO SLIDE: Strike the first note and then slide the same fret-hand finger up or down to the second note. The second note is not struck.

SHIFT SLIDE: Same as legato slide, except the second note is struck.

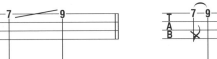

GRACE-NOTE SLUR: Strike the note and immediately hammer-on (pull-off or slide) as indicated.

NATURAL HARMONIC: Strike the note while the fret hand lightly touches the string directly over the fret indicated.

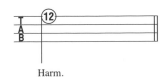

Harm.

MUTED STRING: A percussive sound is produced by laying the fret hand across the string without depressing, and striking it with the pick hand.

Additional Musical Definitions

(staccato) — • Play the note short

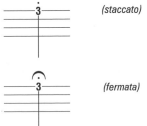

(fermata) — • A hold or pause

D.S. al Coda	• Go back to the sign (%), then play until the measure marked "*To Coda*," then skip to the section labelled "**Coda**."
D.C. al Fine	• Go back to the beginning of the song and play until the measure marked "*Fine*" (end).
Bass Fig.	• Label used to recall a recurring pattern.
N.C.	• No chord
tacet	• Instrument is silent (drops out).

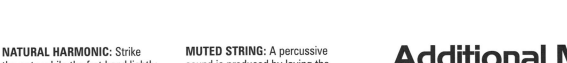

• Repeat measures between signs

• When a repeated section has different endings, play the first ending only the first time and the second ending only the second time.

All the Small Things

Words and Music by Tom DeLonge, Travis Barker and Mark Hoppus

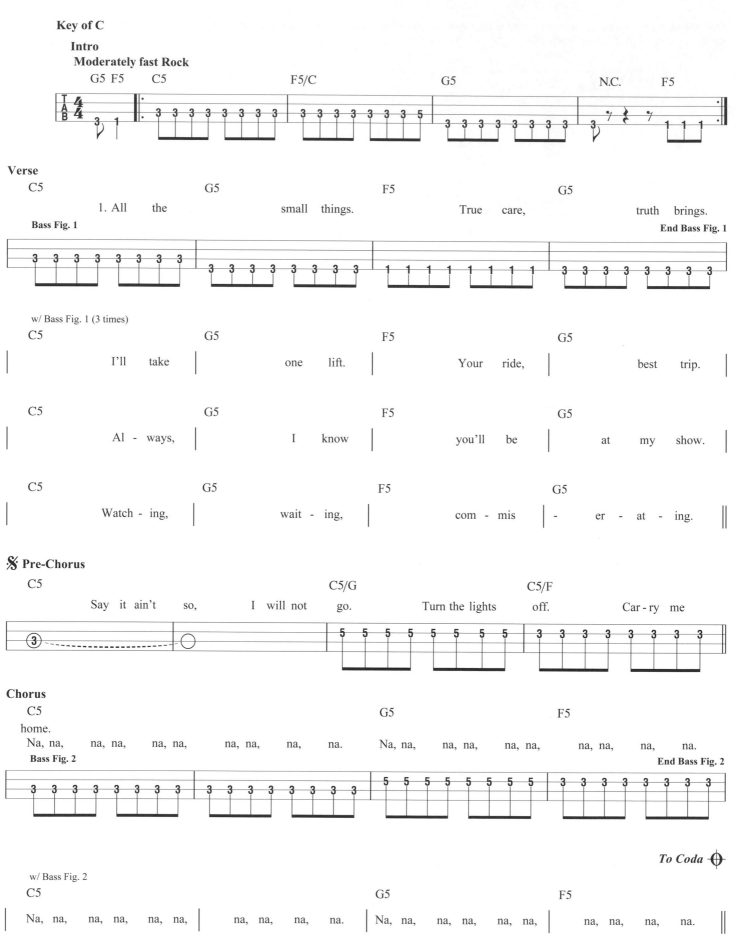

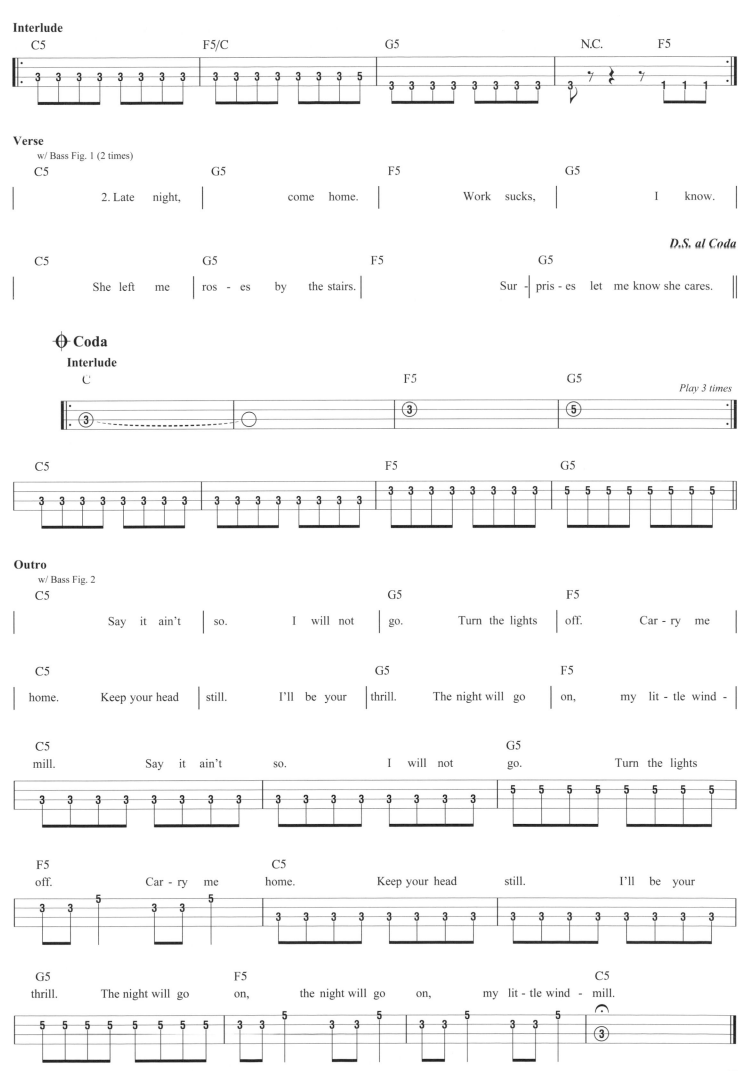

Another Brick in the Wall, Part 2

Words and Music by Roger Waters

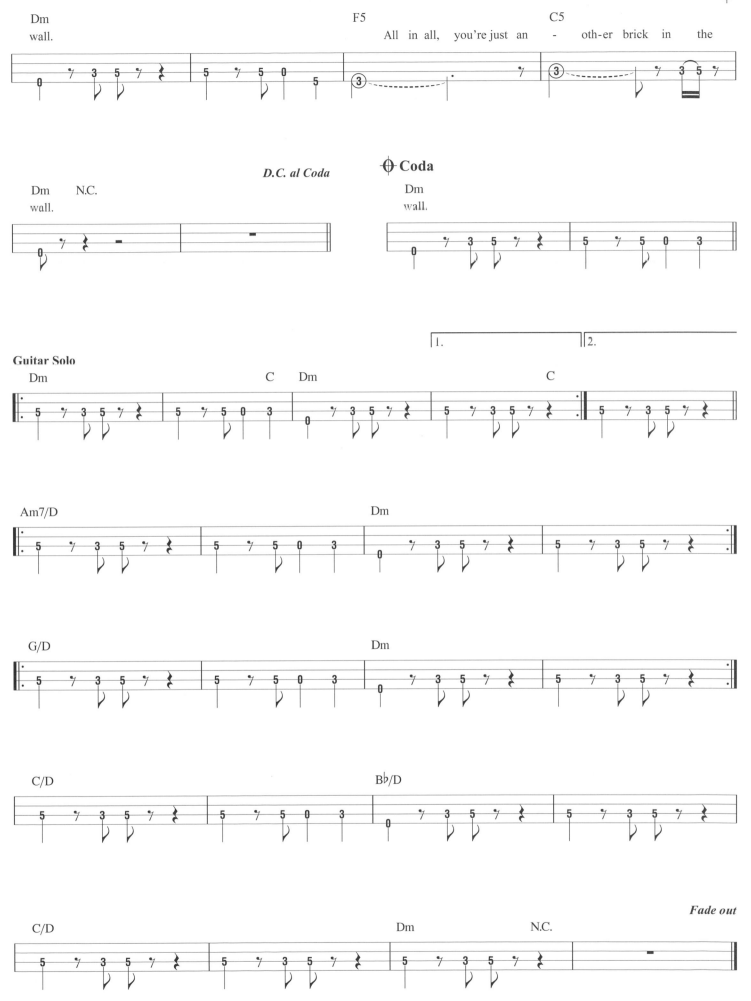

Are You Gonna Be My Girl

Words and Music by Cameron Muncey and Nicholas Cester

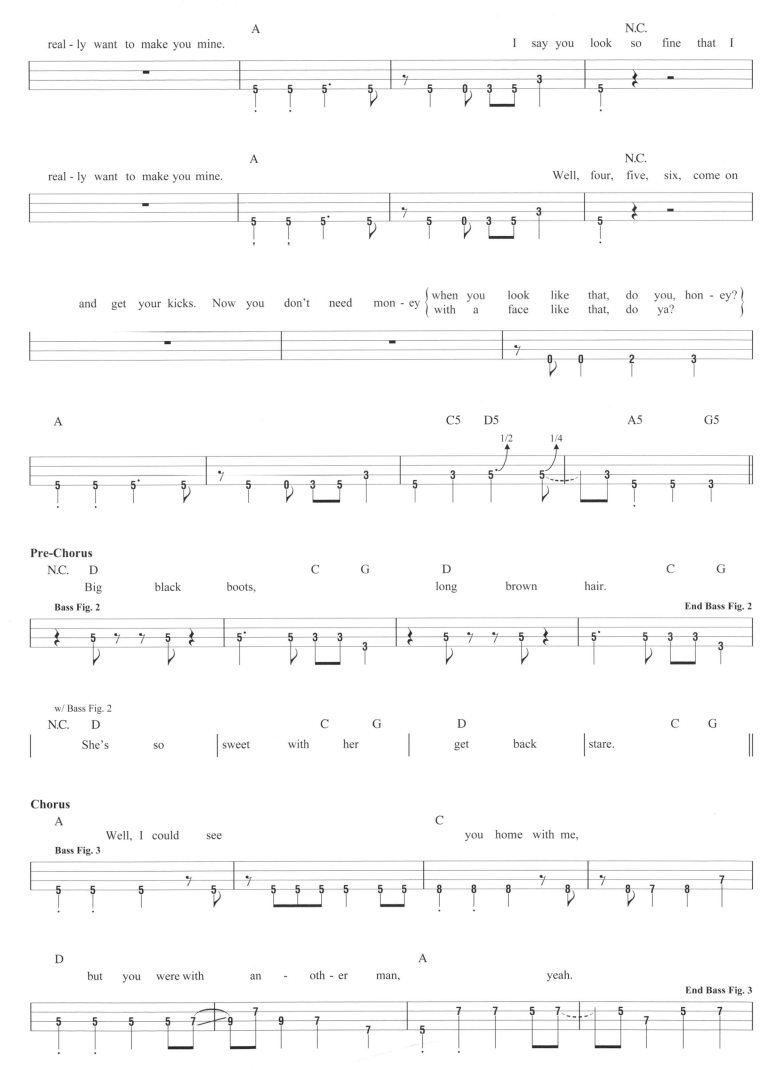

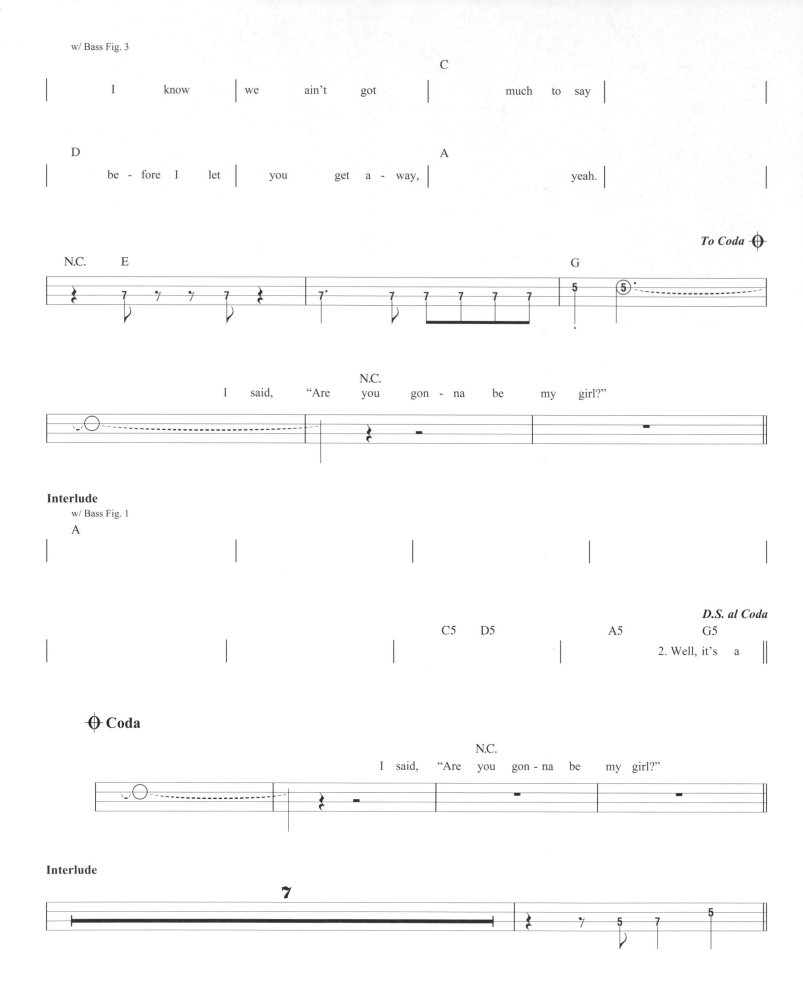

w/ Bass Fig. 3

| I know | we ain't got | C   much to say | |

D
| be - fore I let | you get a - way, | A   yeah. | |

To Coda ⊕

N.C.   E   G

I said, "Are   N.C. you gon - na be   my girl?"

Interlude
w/ Bass Fig. 1
A

D.S. al Coda
C5   D5   A5   G5
                            2. Well, it's a

⊕ **Coda**

N.C.
I said, "Are you gon - na be   my girl?"

Interlude

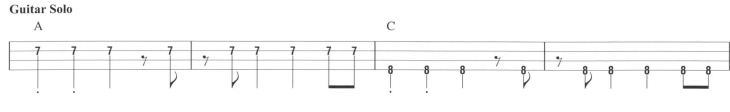

Guitar Solo
A   C

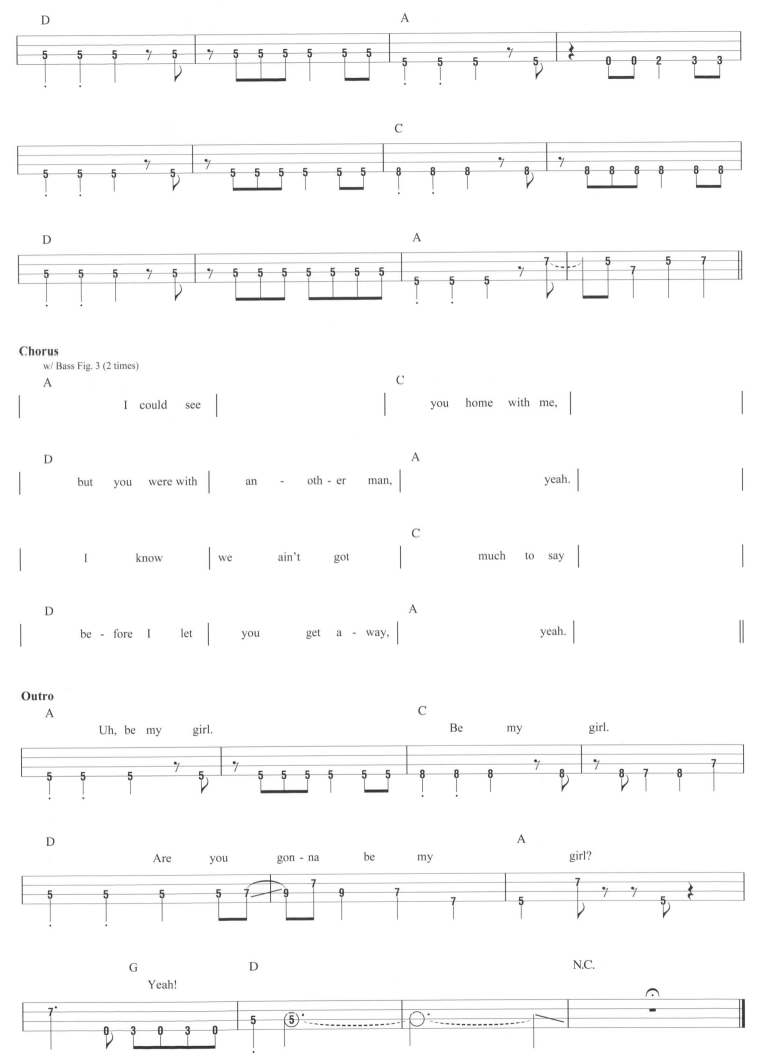

Chorus
w/ Bass Fig. 3 (2 times)

A | I could see | C | you home with me, |

D | but you were with | an - oth - er man, | A | yeah. |

| I know | we ain't got | C | much to say |

D | be - fore I let | you get a - way, | A | yeah. |

Outro

A Uh, be my girl.   C Be my girl.

D Are you gon - na be my A girl?

G Yeah!   D   N.C.

Are You Gonna Go My Way

Words by Lenny Kravitz
Music by Lenny Kravitz and Craig Ross

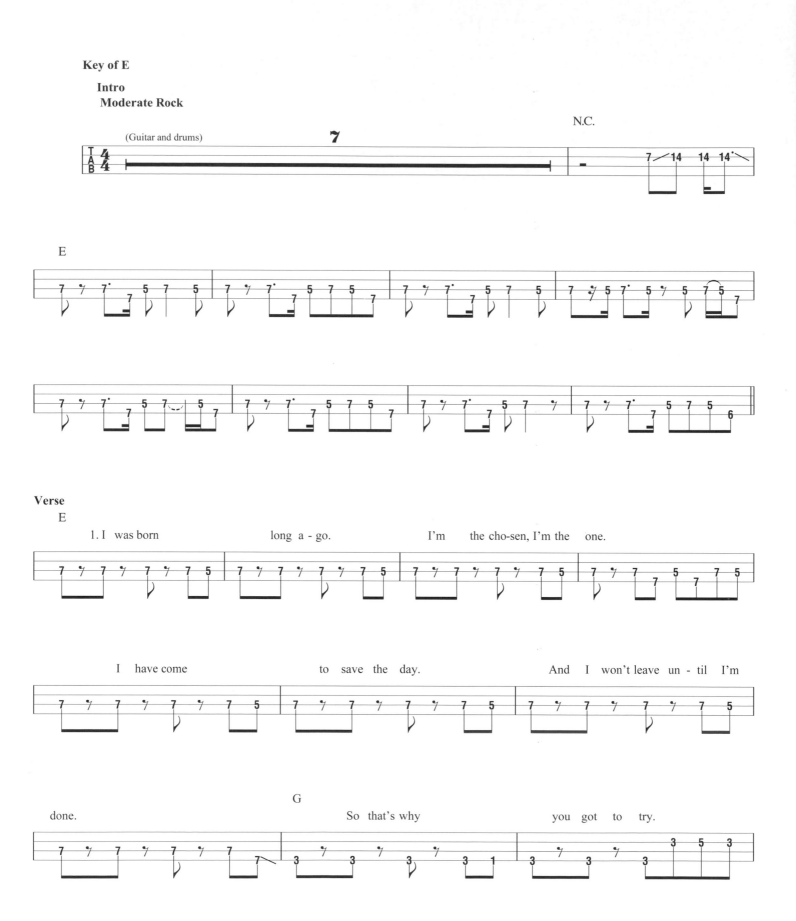

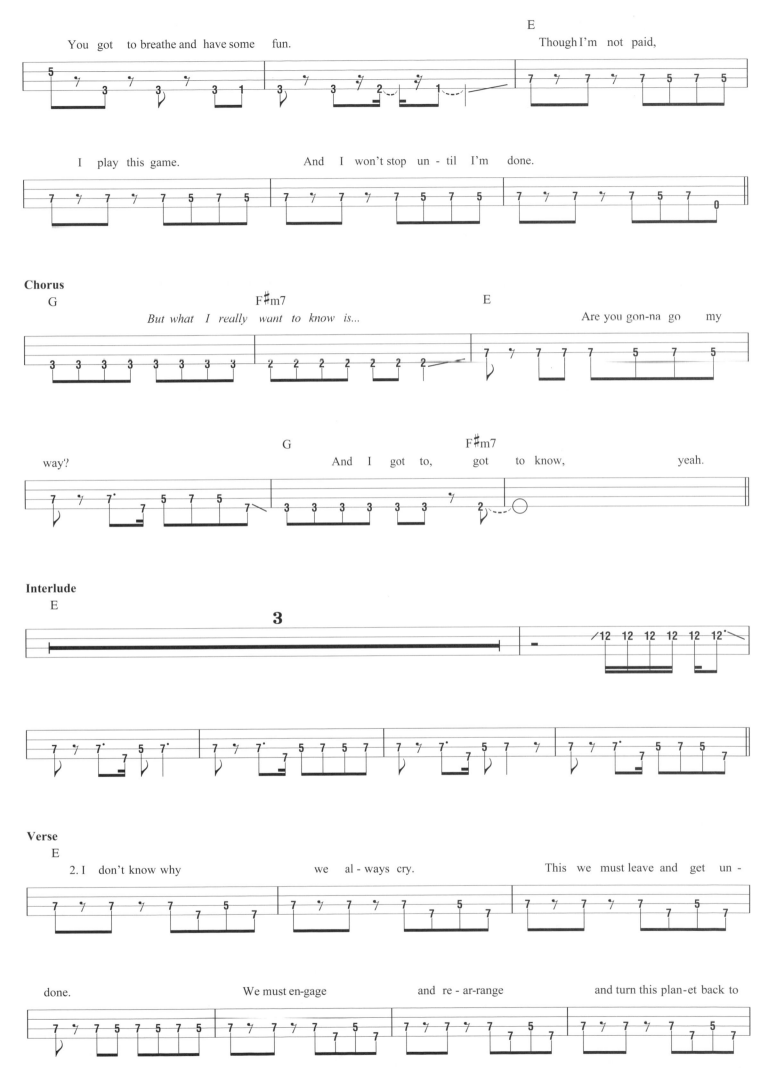

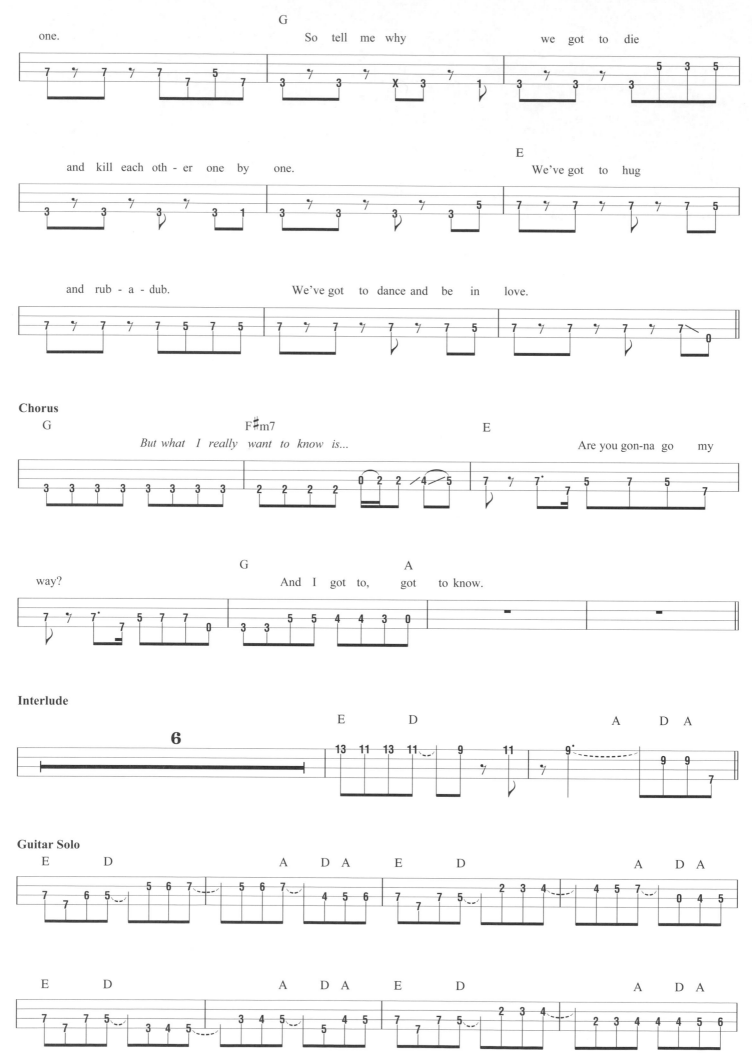

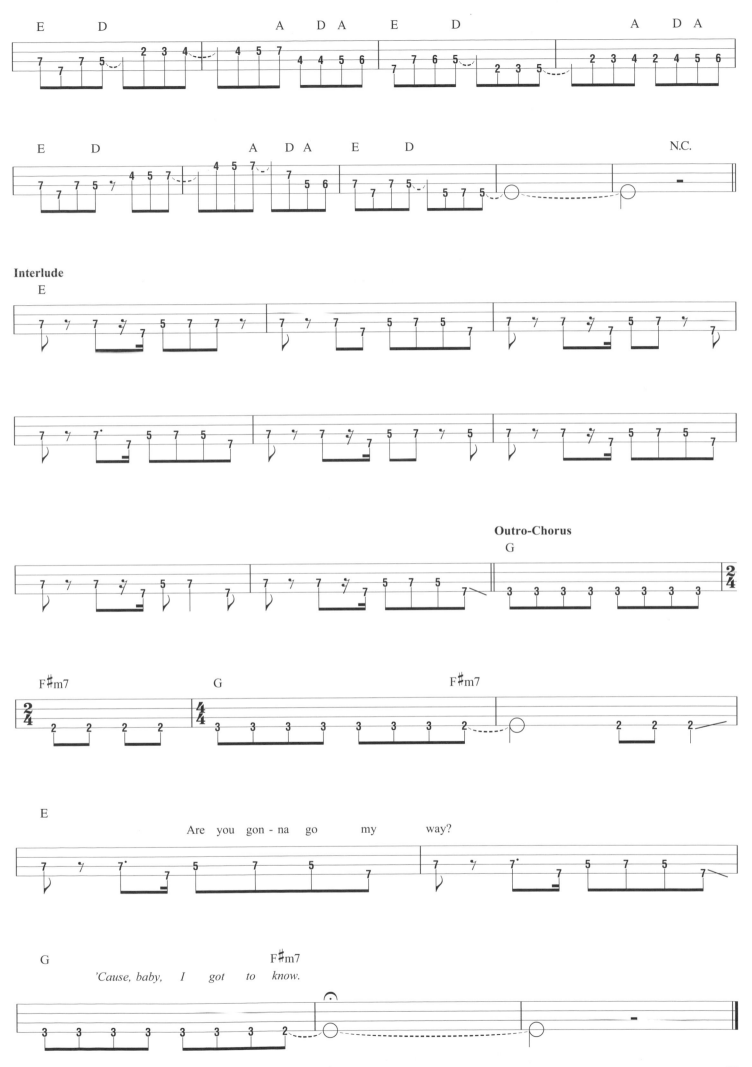

Bad Moon Rising

Words and Music by John Fogerty

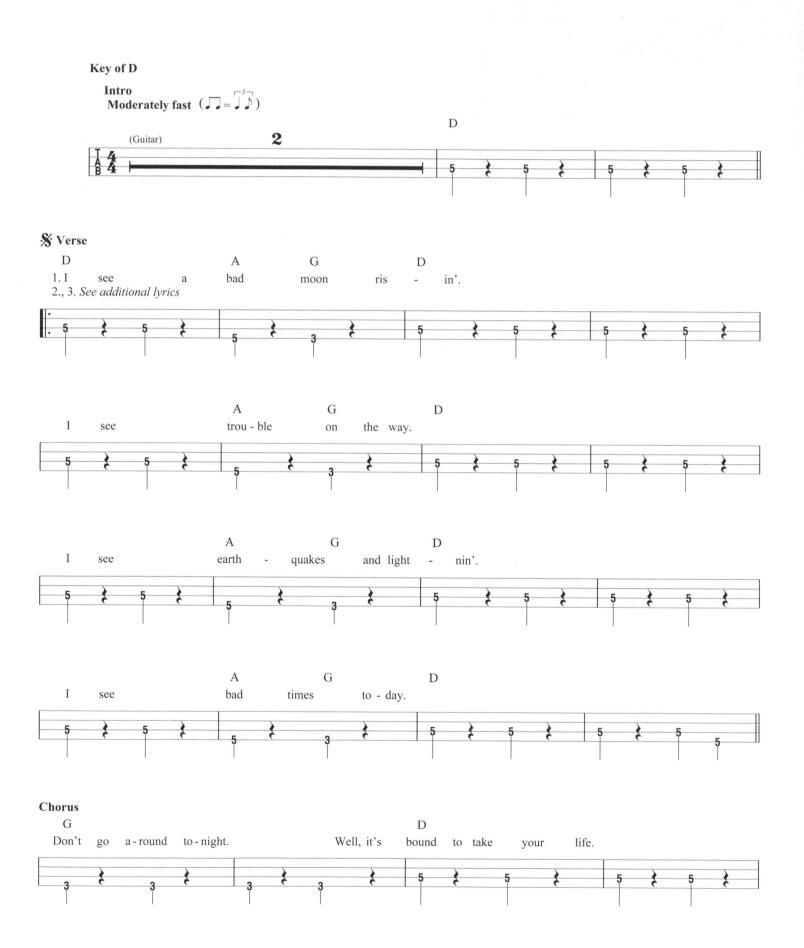

Key of D

Intro
Moderately fast

Verse

1. I see a bad moon ris - in'.
2., 3. *See additional lyrics*

I see trou - ble on the way.

I see earth - quakes and light - nin'.

I see bad times to - day.

Chorus

Don't go a - round to - night. Well, it's bound to take your life.

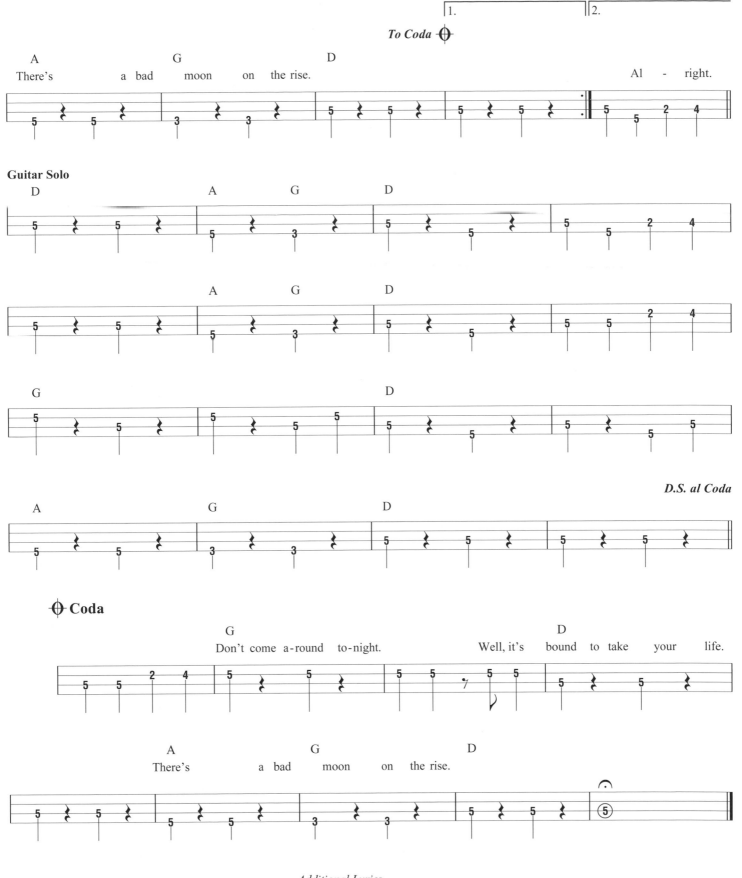

Additional Lyrics

2. I hear hurricanes a blowin'.
   I know the end is comin' soon.
   I fear rivers overflowin'.
   I hear the voice of rage and ruin.

3. Hope you got your things together.
   Hope you are quite prepared to die.
   Looks like we're in for nasty weather.
   One eye is taken for an eye. Well...

By the Way

Words and Music by Anthony Kiedis, Flea, John Frusciante and Chad Smith

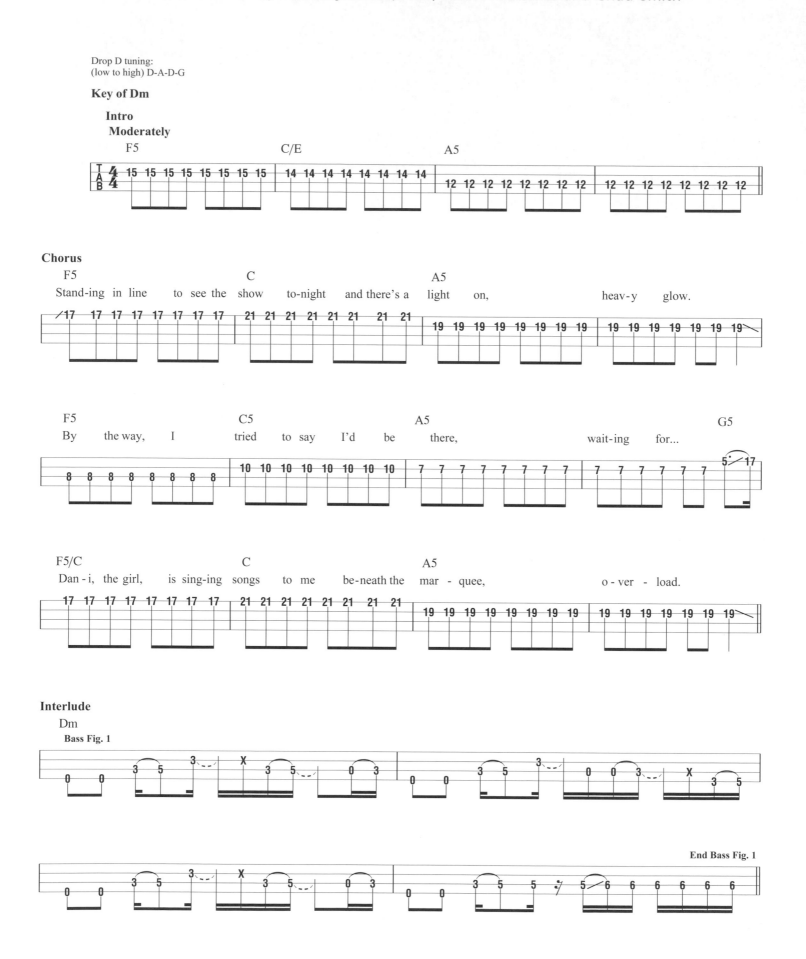

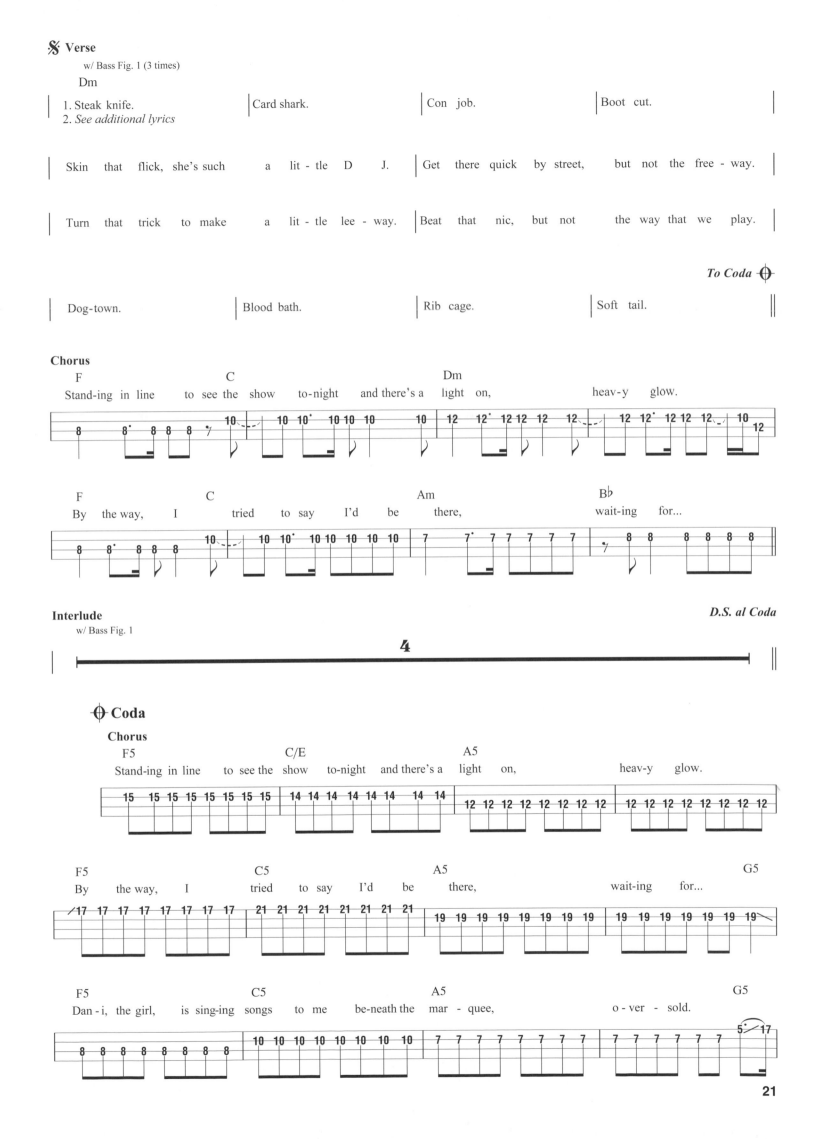

𝄋 Verse

w/ Bass Fig. 1 (3 times)

Dm

| 1. Steak knife. | Card shark. | Con job. | Boot cut. |

2. *See additional lyrics*

| Skin that flick, she's such | a lit - tle D J. | Get there quick by street, | but not the free - way. |

| Turn that trick to make | a lit - tle lee - way. | Beat that nic, but not | the way that we play. |

To Coda ⊕

| Dog-town. | Blood bath. | Rib cage. | Soft tail. |

Chorus

F   C   Dm

Stand-ing in line   to see the show   to-night   and there's a   light on,   heav-y   glow.

F   C   Am   B♭

By   the way,   I   tried   to   say   I'd   be   there,   wait-ing   for...

Interlude   *D.S. al Coda*

w/ Bass Fig. 1

4

⊕ **Coda**

Chorus

F5   C/E   A5

Stand-ing in line   to see the   show   to-night   and there's a   light   on,   heav-y   glow.

F5   C5   A5   G5

By   the way,   I   tried   to   say   I'd   be   there,   wait-ing   for...

F5   C5   A5   G5

Dan - i, the girl,   is sing-ing   songs   to me   be-neath the   mar - quee,   o - ver - sold.

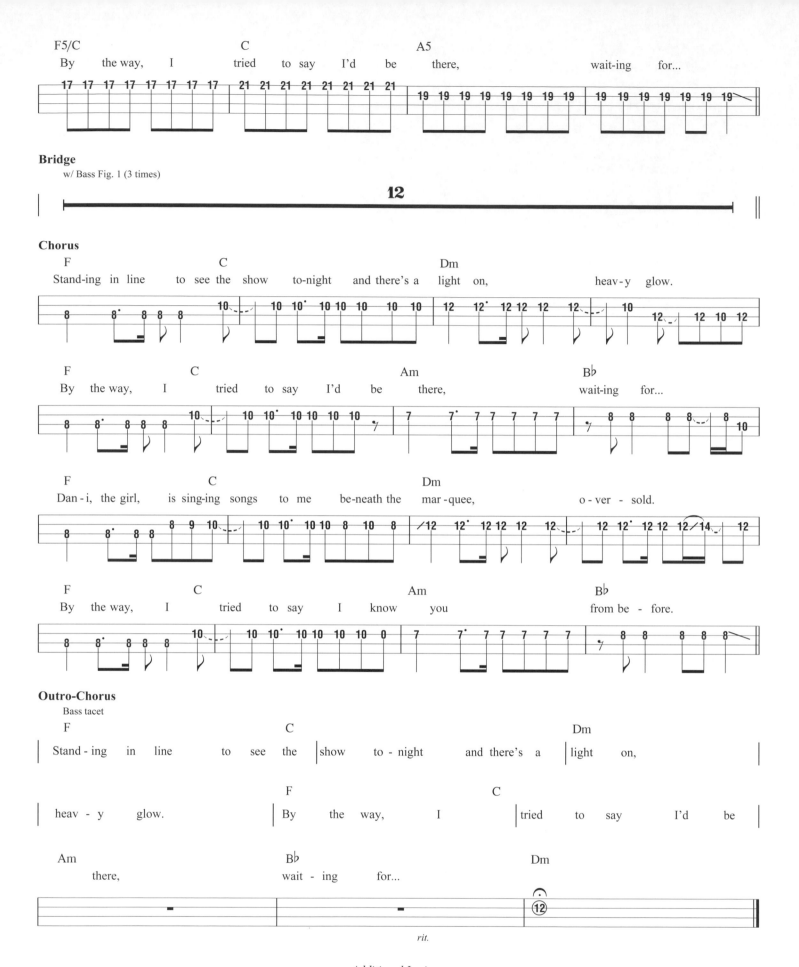

Outro-Chorus

Bass tacet

rit.

Additional Lyrics

2. *Spoken: Blackjack. Dope dick. Pawn shop. Quick pick.*
Kiss that dyke, I know you want to hold one.
Not on strike, but I'm about to bowl one.
Bite that mic, I know you never stole one.
Girls that like a story, so I told one.
Song bird. Main line. Cash back. Hard top.

Can't Stop the Feeling!

from TROLLS

Words and Music by Justin Timberlake, Max Martin and Shellback

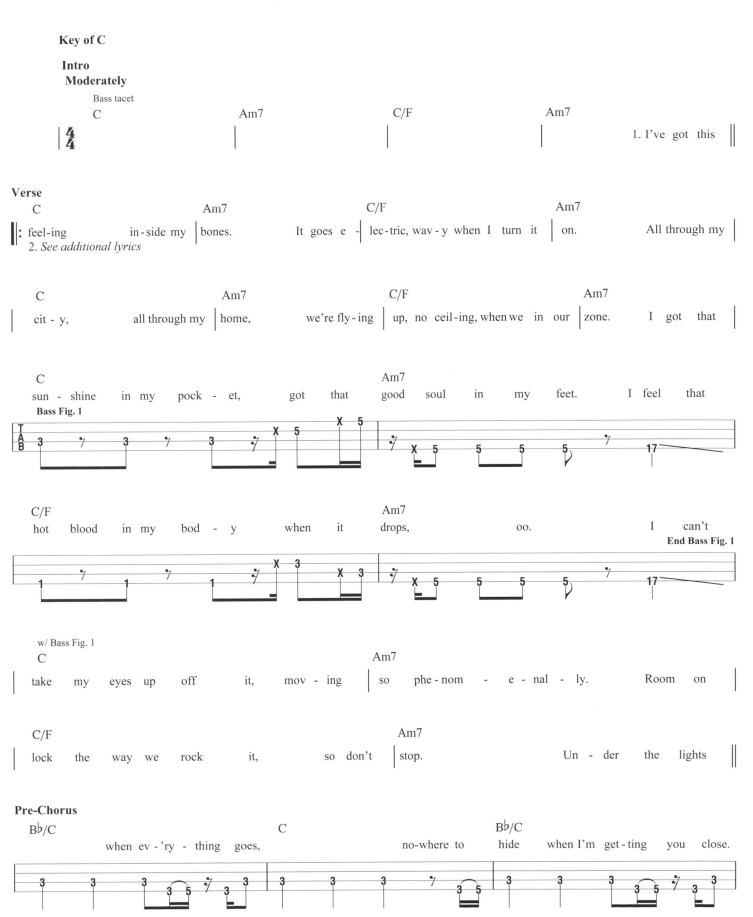

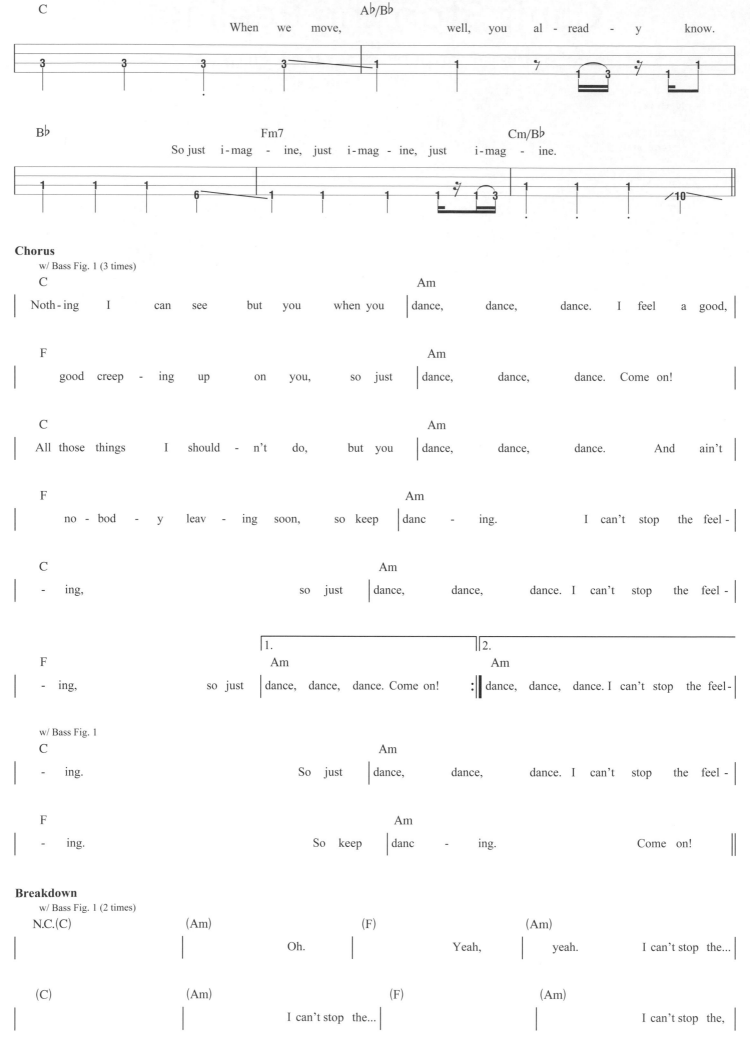

Chorus

w/ Bass Fig. 1 (4 times)

C

I can't stop the, I can't stop the feel... | Noth-ing I can see but you when you

Am   F

dance, dance, dance. I feel a good, | good creep - ing up on you, so just

Am   C

dance, dance, dance. Come on! | All those things I should - n't do, but you

Am   F

dance, dance, dance. And ain't | no - bod - y leav - ing soon, so keep

Am   C

danc - ing. I can't stop the feel | - ing. Got this feel - ing in my

Am   F

bod - y. I can't stop the feel | - ing. Got this feel - ing in my

Am   C

bod - y. I can't stop the feel | - ing. Wan - na see you move your

Am   F

bod - y. I can't stop the feel | - ing. Got this feel - ing in my

Bass tacet

Am   N.C.

bod - y. Break it | down! Got this feel - ing in my

bod - y. Can't stop the feel | - ing. Got this feel - ing in my

bod - y. Come on! |

Additional Lyrics

2. Ooh, it's something magical.
 It's in the air, it's in my blood, it's rushing on.
 I don't need no reason, don't need control.
 I fly so high, no ceiling, when I'm in my zone.
 'Cause I got that...

Cake by the Ocean

Words and Music by Joseph Jonas, Justin Tranter, Robin Fredriksson and Mattias Larsson

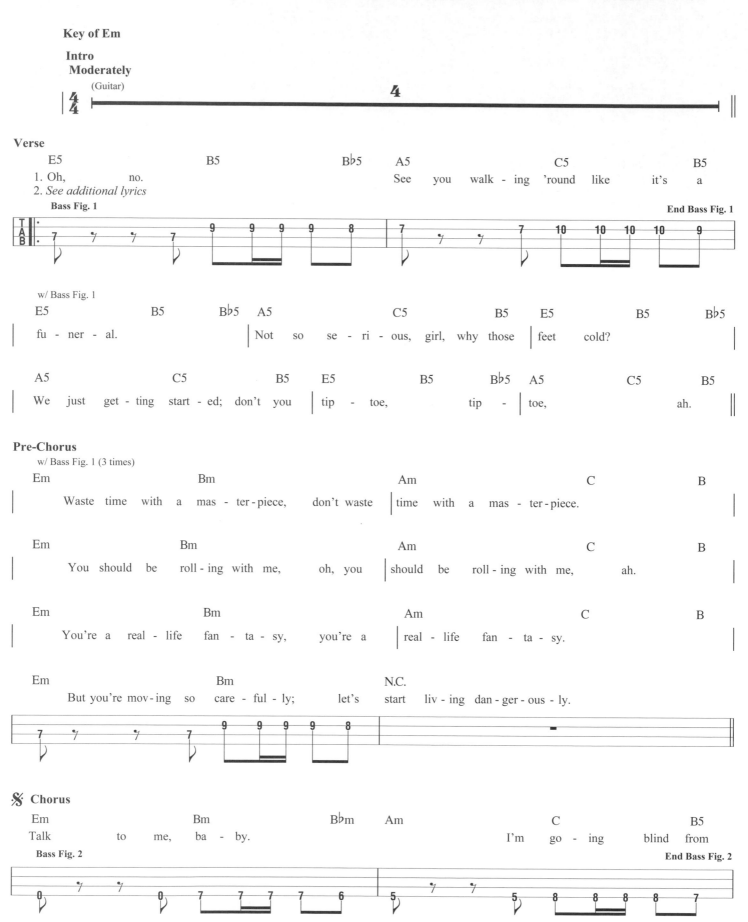

w/ Bass Fig. 2 (7 times)

Em	Bm	B♭m	Am		C	B	Em	Bm	B♭m

this   sweet, sweet crav - ing, whoa, oh.   Let's lose our minds and   go   fuck - ing cra - zy.

Am	C	B	Em	Bm	B♭m	Am	C	B

Ah, ya, ya, ya, ya.   I   keep on hop - ing we'll eat   cake   by   the o - cean, huh.

Em	Bm	B♭m	Am	C	B	Em	Bm	B♭m

Walk   for   me, ba - by.   I'll be Did - dy,   you'll   be   Na - o - mi, whoa, oh.

Am	C	B	Em	Bm	B♭m	Am	C	B

Let's lose our minds and   go   fuck - ing cra - zy.   Ah, ya, ya, ya, ya.

1.

To Coda ⊕

Interlude
Bass tacet

Em	Bm	B♭m	Am	C	B

I   keep on hop - ing we'll eat   cake   by   the   o - cean, huh.

2

2.

w/ Bass Fig. 2 (4 times)

Em	Bm	B♭m	Am	C	B	Em	Bm	B♭m

Ah, ya, ya, ya, ya.   I   keep on hop - ing we'll eat

Am	C	B	Em	Bm	B♭m	Am	C	B

cake   by   the   o - cean, huh.   Ah, ya, ya, ya, ya.

Interlude
Bass tacet

Em	Bm	B♭m	Am	C	B	E5	B5	B♭5

I   keep on hop - ing we'll eat   cake   by   the   o - cean, huh.   Hey.

D.S. al Coda

A5	C5	B5	E5	B5	B♭5	N.C.

You're fuck - in' de - li - cious.   Ha, ha, ha.   Talk   to   me,   girl.

⊕ **Coda**

Outro
w/ Bass Fig. 2 (4 times)

Em	Bm	B♭m	Am	C	B

Red   vel - vet,   va - nil - la,   choc - 'late   in   my   life.

Em	Bm	B♭m	Am	C	B	Em	Bm	B♭m

Con - fet - ti, I'm read - y,   I need it ev - 'ry night.   Red   vel - vet,   va -

Am	C	B	Em	Bm	B♭m	Am	C	B

nil - la... Ah, ya, ya, ya, ya.   I   keep on hop - ing we'll eat   cake   by   the   o - cean, huh.

Additional Lyrics

2. God damn! See you lickin' frosting from your own hands.
   Want another taste? I'm beggin', "Yes, ma'am."
   I'm tired of all this candy on the dry land, dry land, oh.

Can't You See

Words and Music by Toy Caldwell

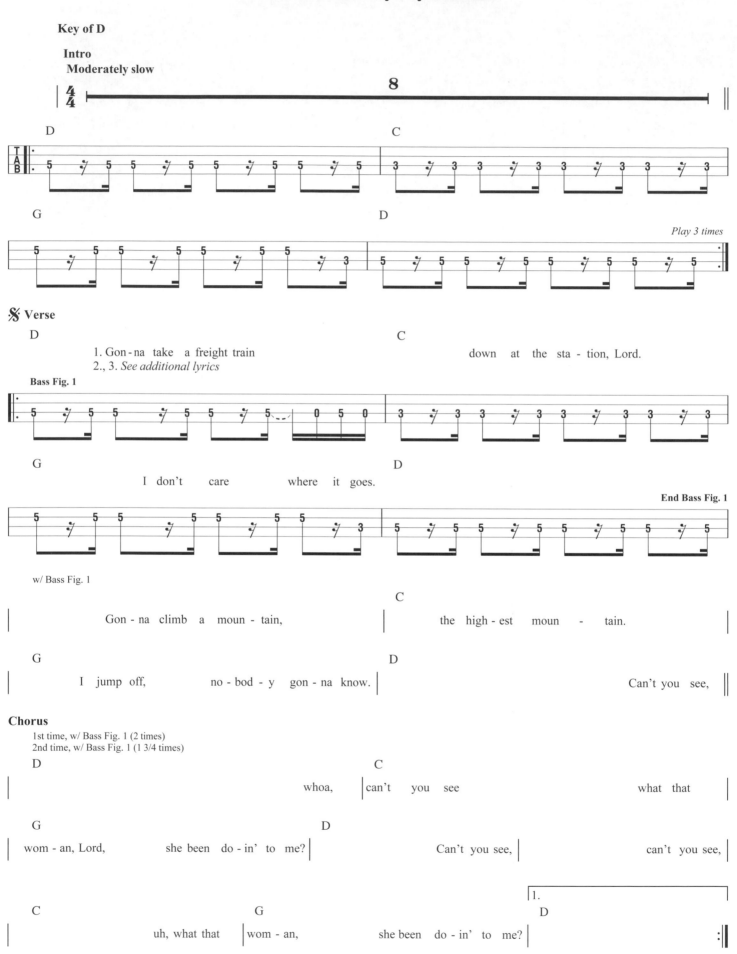

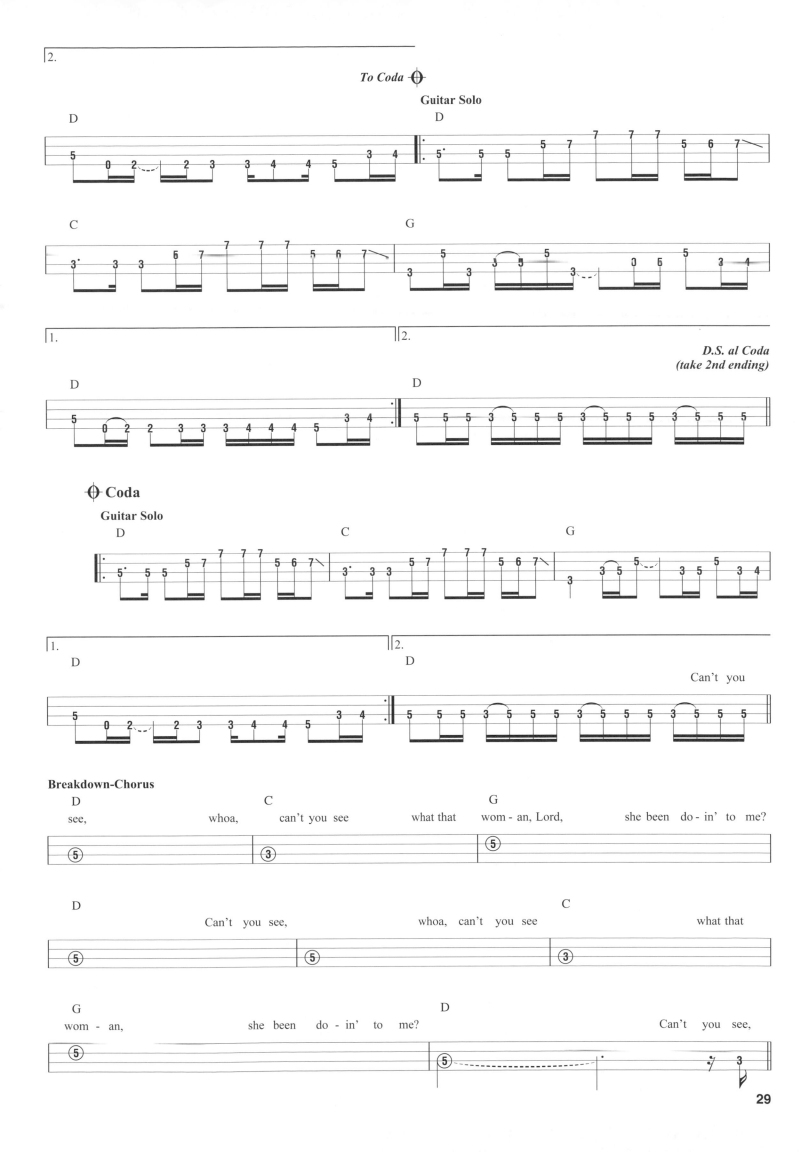

Chorus

w/ Bass Fig. 1 (3 3/4 times)

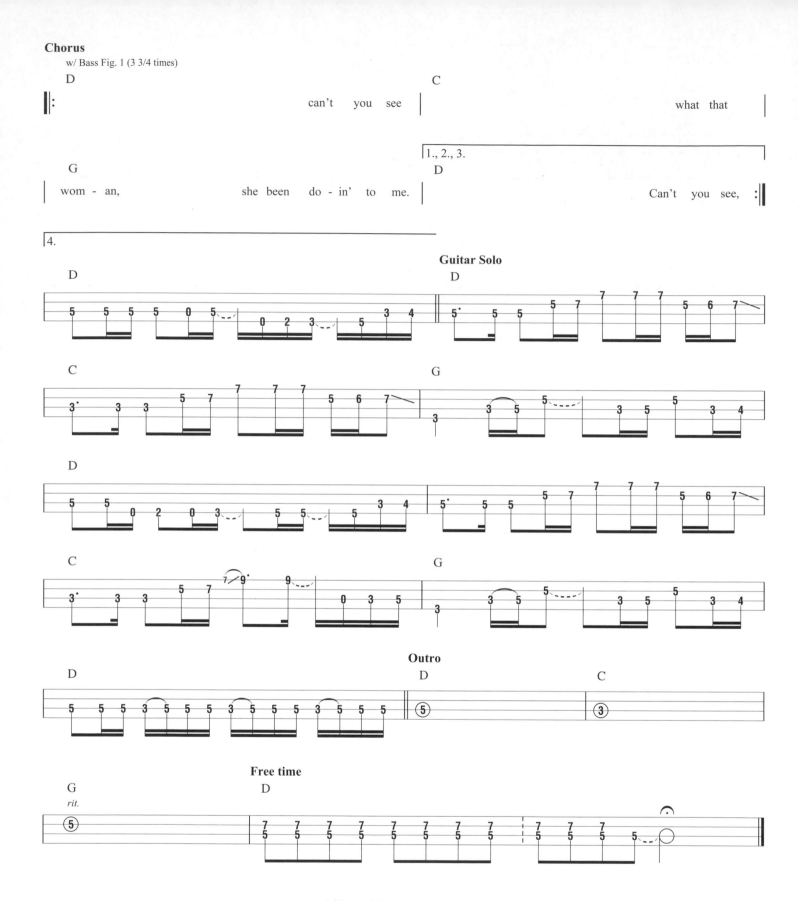

Additional Lyrics

2. I'm gonna find me a hole in the wall.
   I'm gonna crawl inside and die.
   Come later now, a mean old woman, Lord,
   Never told me goodbye.

3. I'm gonna buy a ticket, now, as far as I can.
   Ain't never comin' back.
   Grab me a southbound, oh, all the way to Georgia now,
   Till the train, it run out of track.

Every Breath You Take

Music and Lyrics by Sting

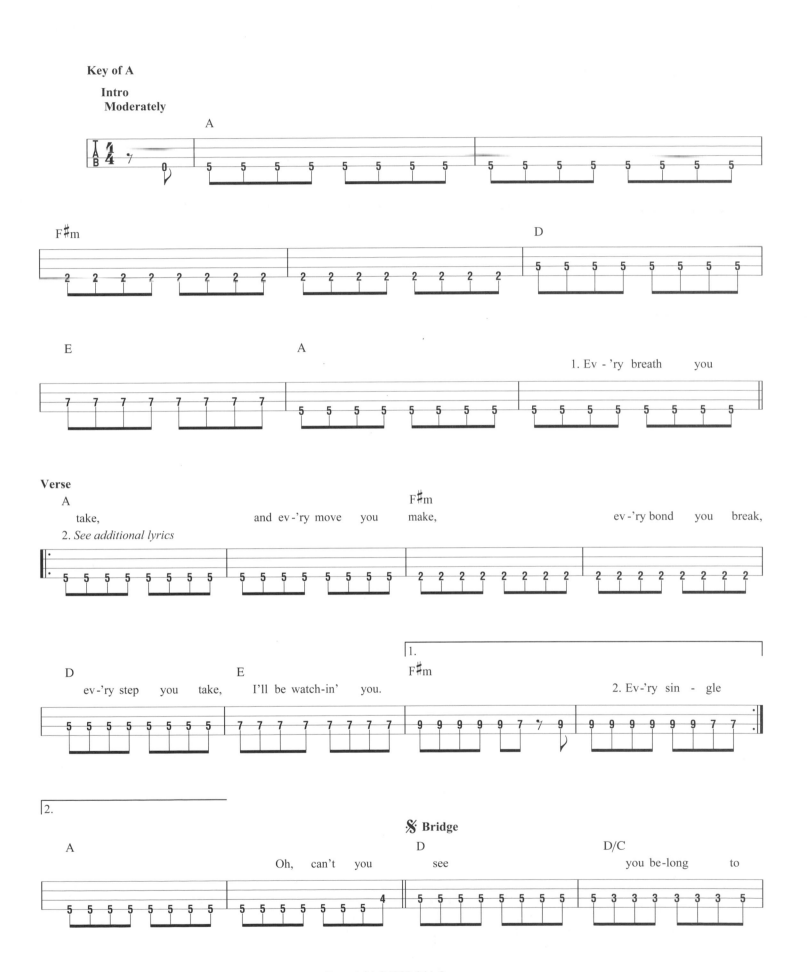

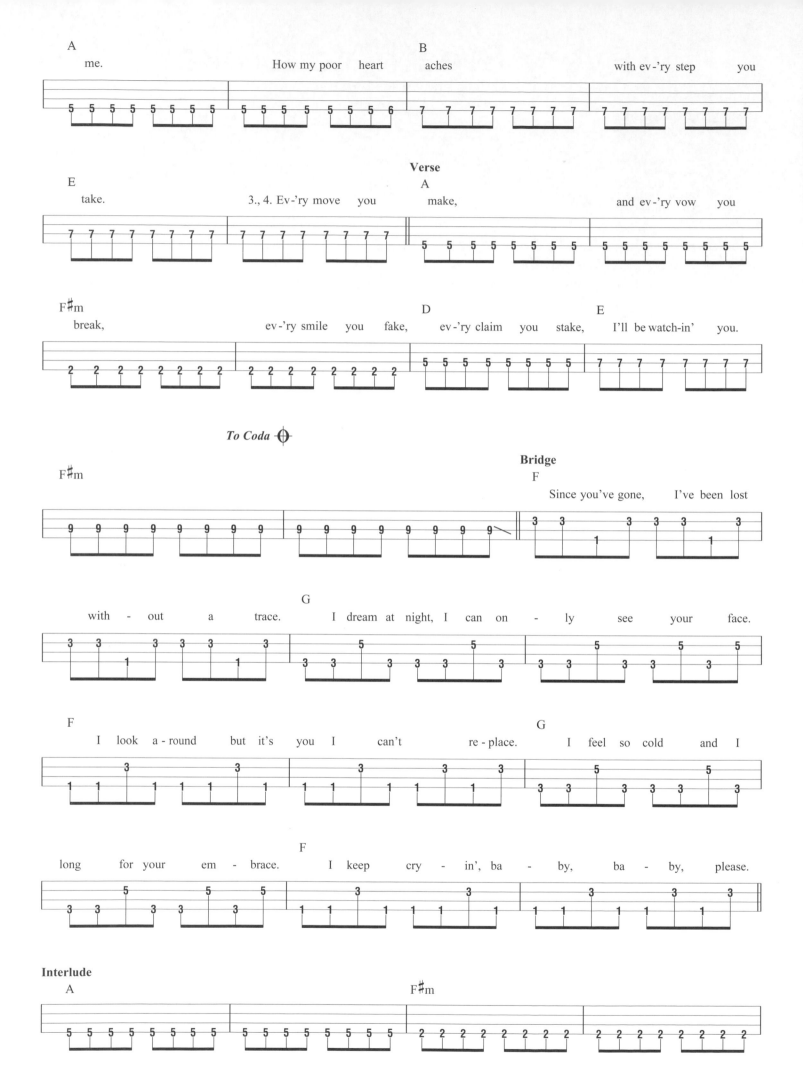

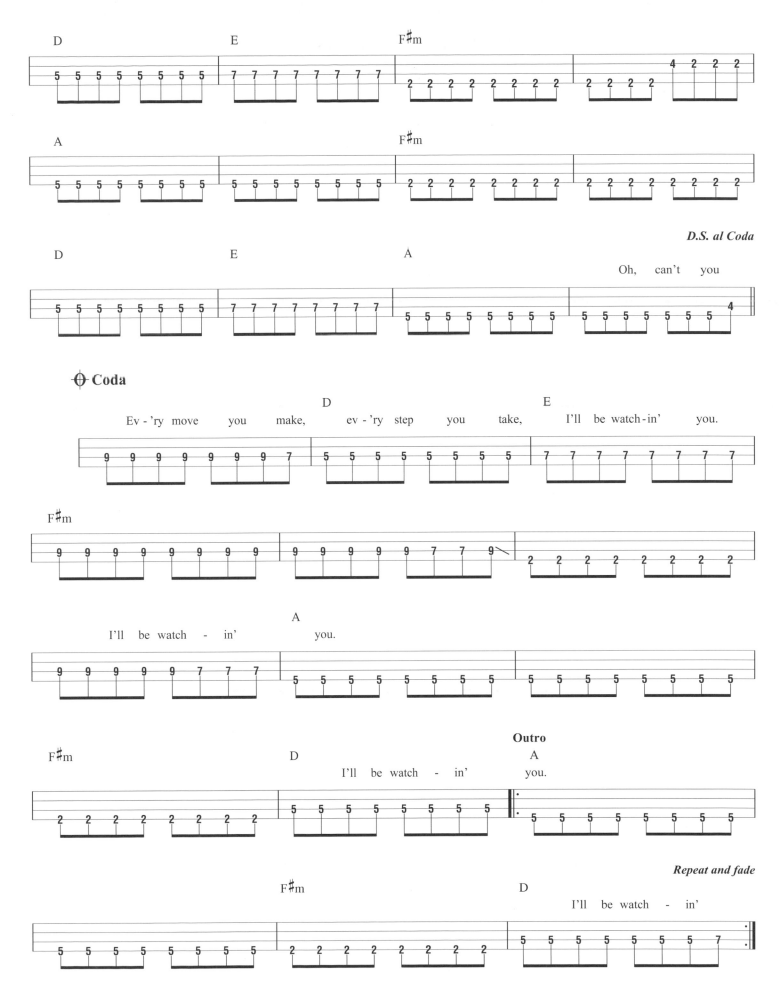

Additional Lyrics

2. Ev'ry single day, and ev'ry word you say,
   Ev'ry game you play, ev'ry night you stay,
   I'll be watchin' you.

Come Together

Words and Music by John Lennon and Paul McCartney

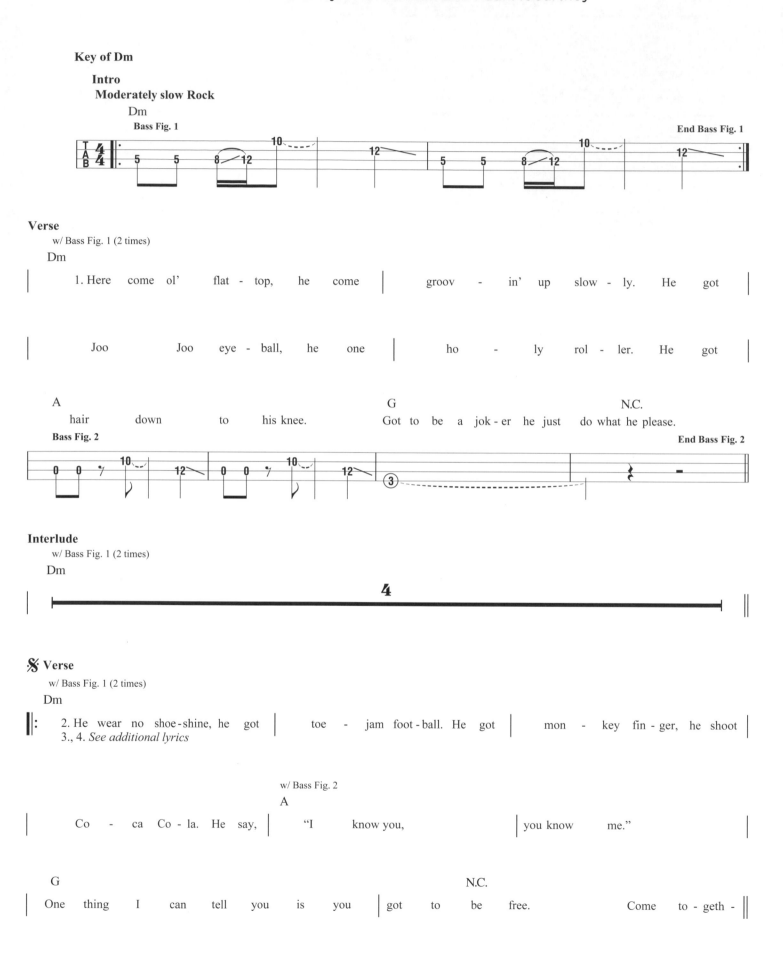

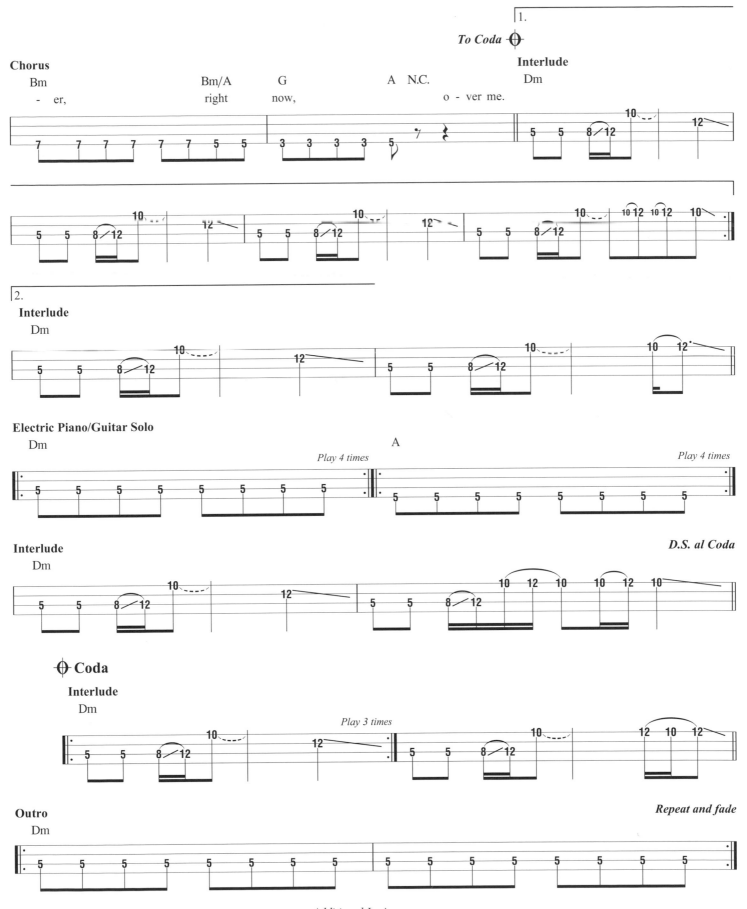

Additional Lyrics

3. He bag production, he got walrus gumboot.
   He got ono sideboard, he one spinal cracker.
   He got feet down below his knee.
   Hold you in his armchair, you can feel his disease.

4. He rollercoaster, he got early warning.
   He got muddy water, he one Mojo filter,
   He say, "One and one and one is three."
   Got to be good lookin' 'cause he's so hard to see.

Free Fallin'

Words and Music by Tom Petty and Jeff Lynne

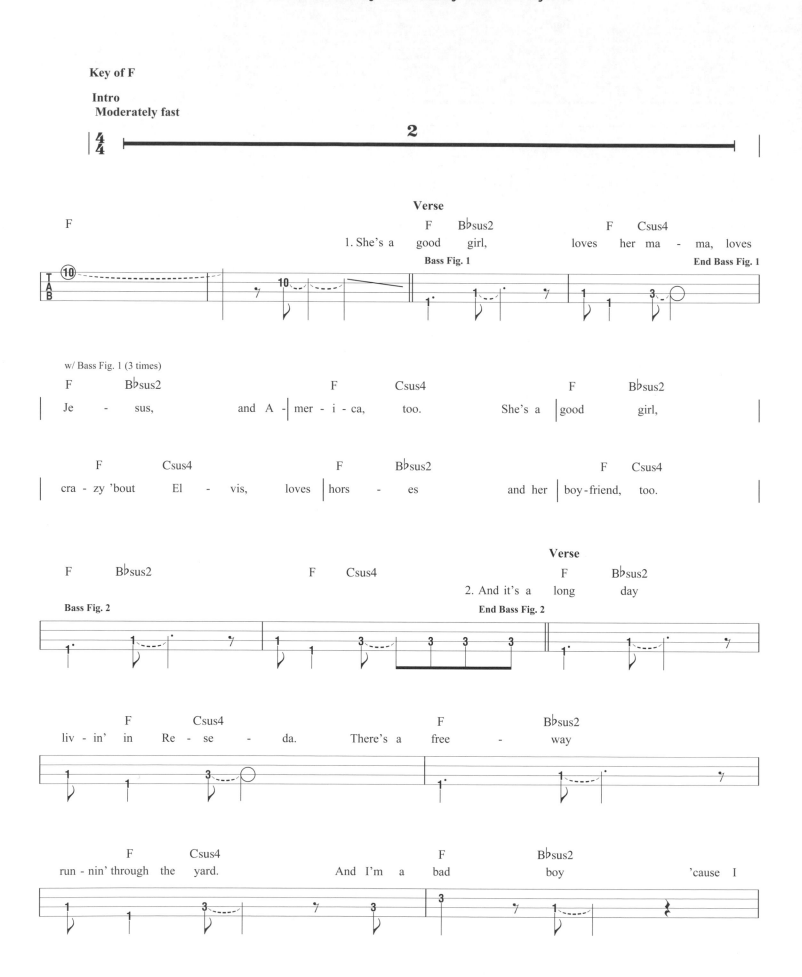

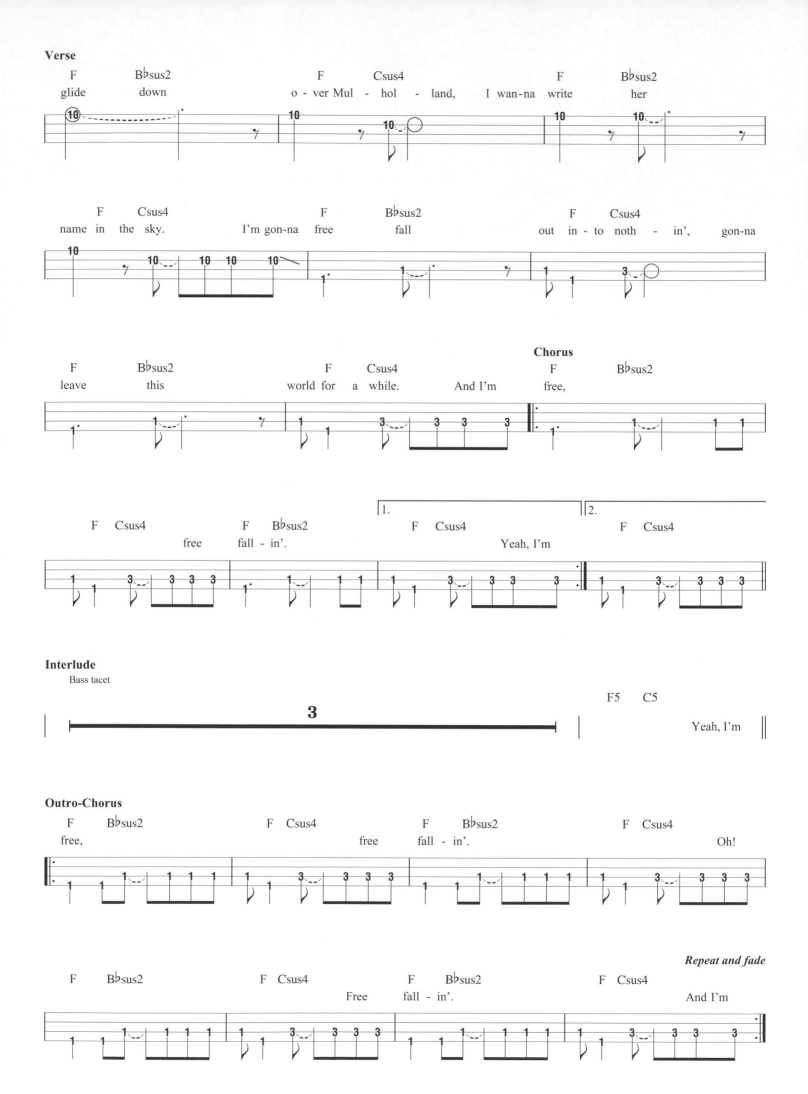

Gimme Some Lovin'

Words and Music by Steve Winwood, Muff Winwood and Spencer Davis

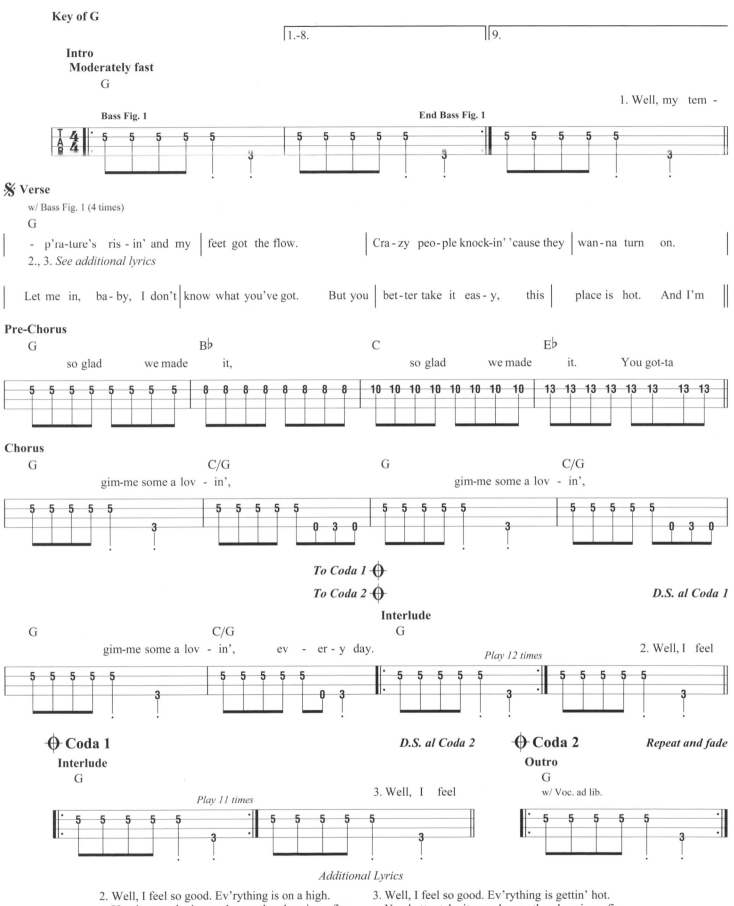

Additional Lyrics

2. Well, I feel so good. Ev'rything is on a high.
   You better take it easy 'cause the place is on fire.
   It's been a hard day and I had some work to do.
   We made it baby, and it happened to you.

3. Well, I feel so good. Ev'rything is gettin' hot.
   You better take it easy 'cause the place is on fire.
   It's been a hard day, nothin' went too good.
   Now I'm gonna relax, honey. Ev'rybody should.

Highway to Hell

Words and Music by Angus Young, Malcolm Young and Bon Scott

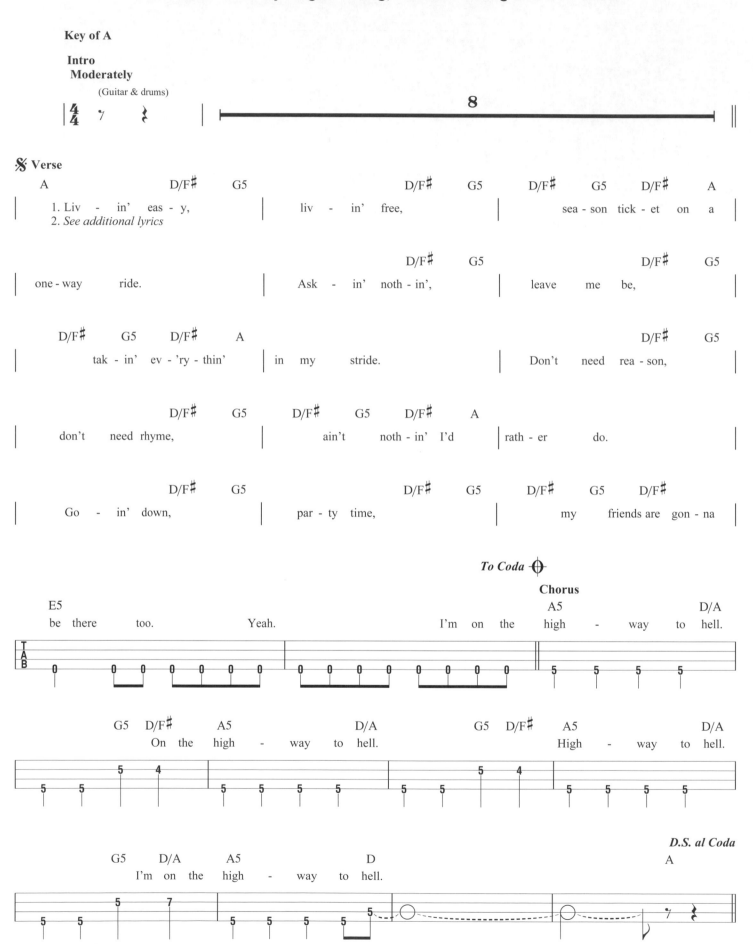

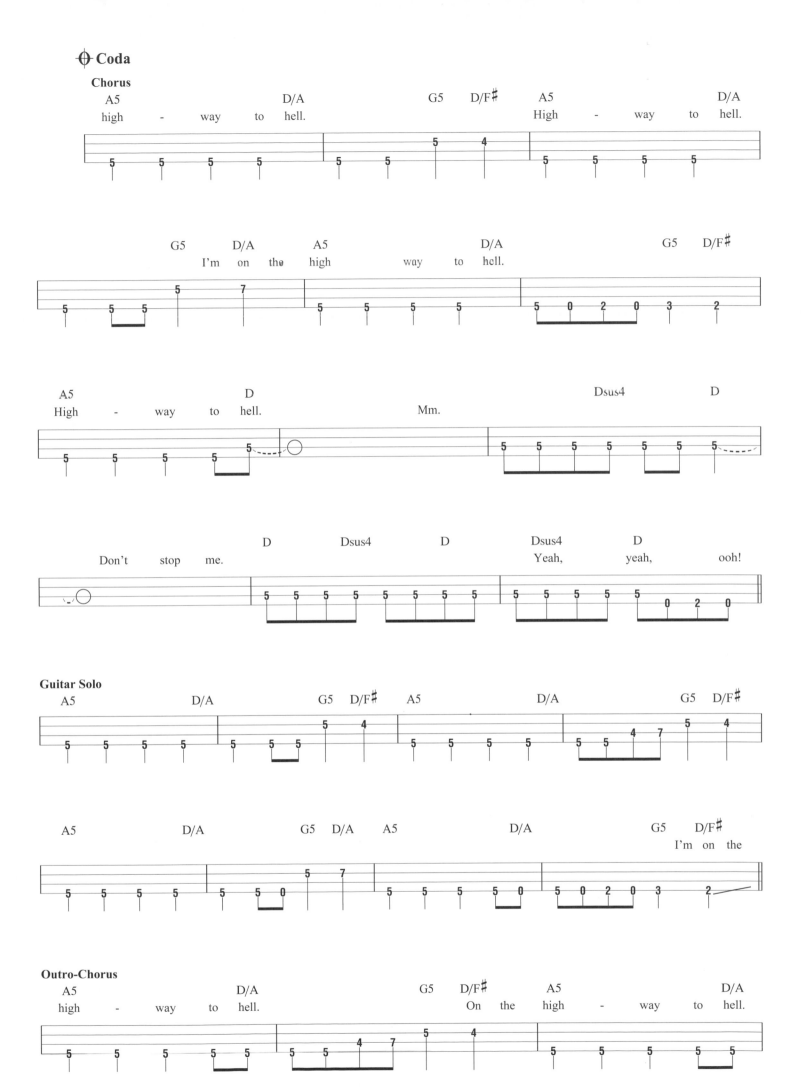

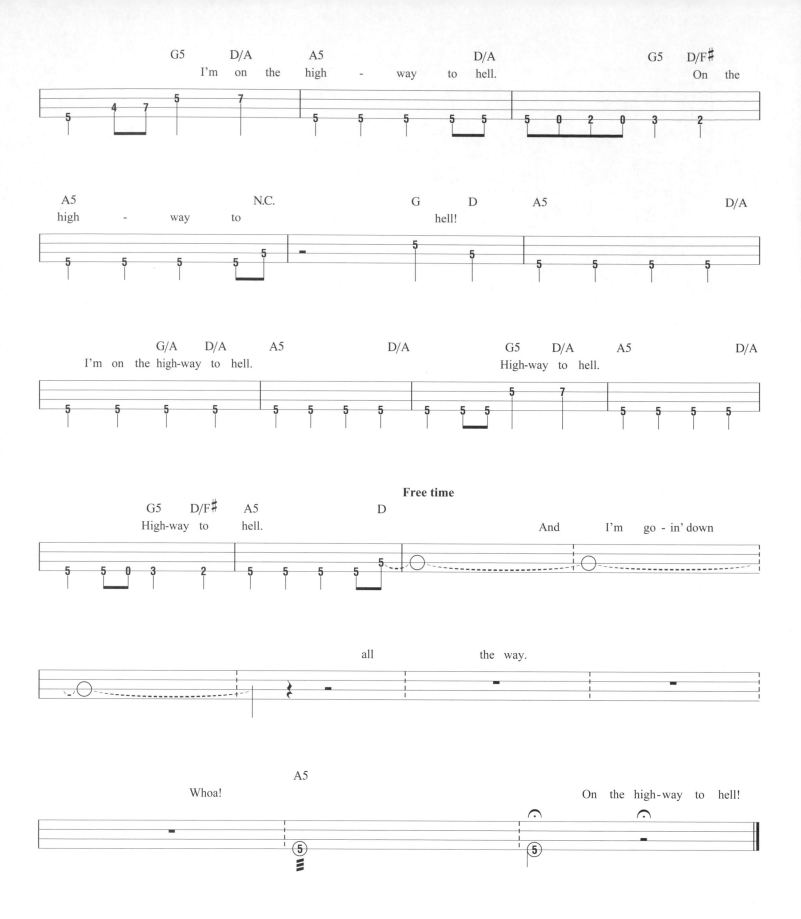

Additional Lyrics

2. No stop signs, speed limit, nobody's gonna slow me down.
   Like a wheel, gonna spin it, nobody's gonna mess me around.
   Hey Satan, pay'n' my dues, playin' in a rockin' band.
   Hey mama, look at me, I'm on my way to the promised land. Whoa!

No Excuses

Words and Music by Jerry Cantrell

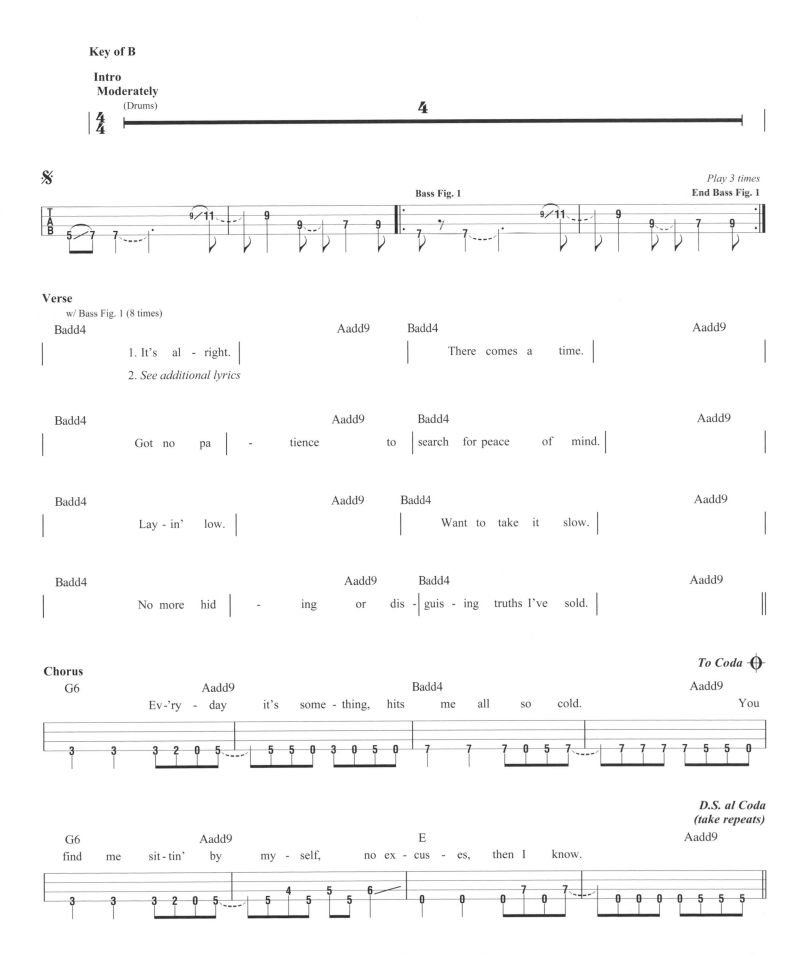

Coda

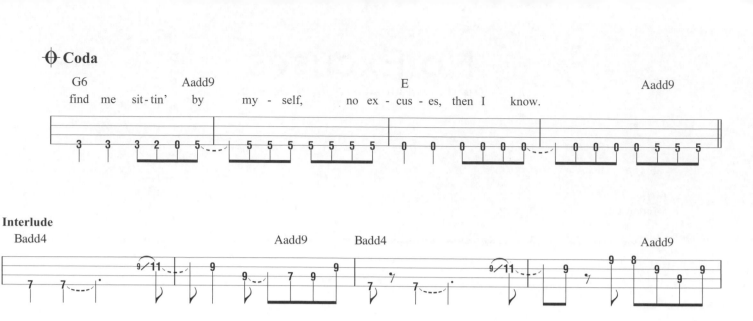

Interlude

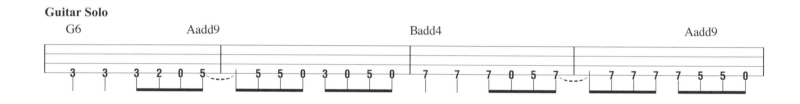

Guitar Solo

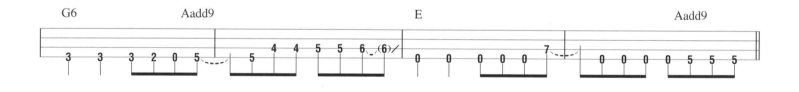

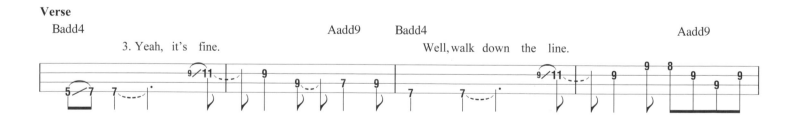

Verse

3. Yeah, it's fine.   Well, walk down the line.

Leave our rain,   a cold trade for warm sun-shine.

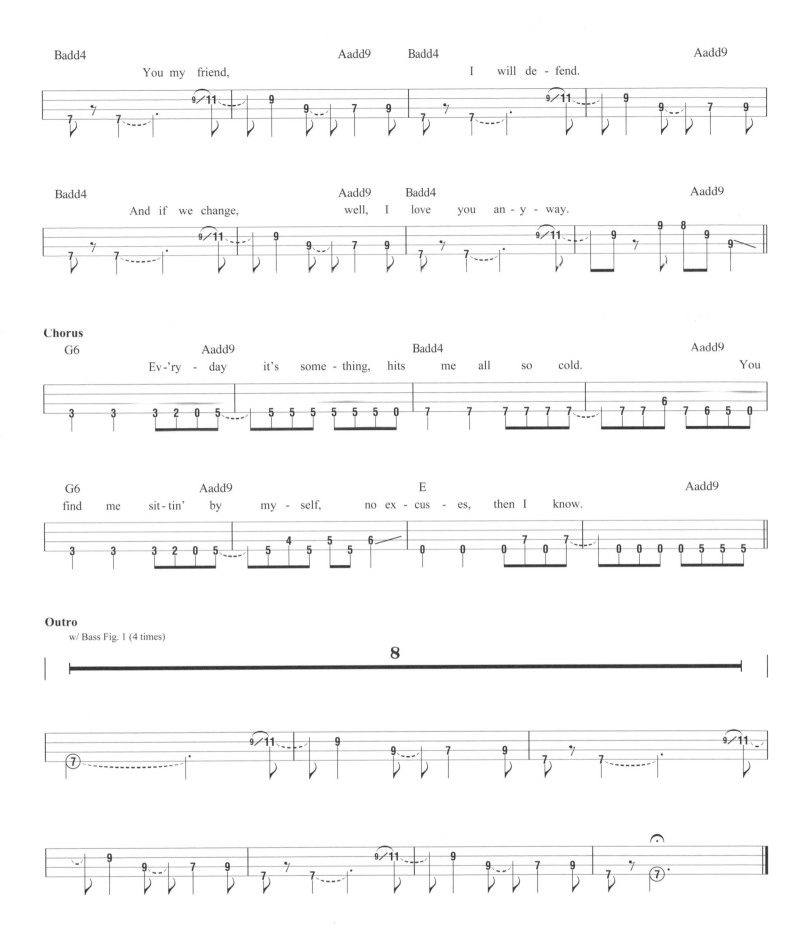

Outro

w/ Bass Fig. 1 (4 times)

Additional Lyrics

2. It's okay. Had a bad day.
   Hands are bruised from breaking rocks all day.
   Drained and blue, I bleed for you.
   You think it's funny, well, you're drowning in it too.

I Gotta Feeling

Words and Music by Will Adams, Allan Pineda, Jaime Gomez,
Stacy Ferguson, David Guetta and Frederic Riesterer

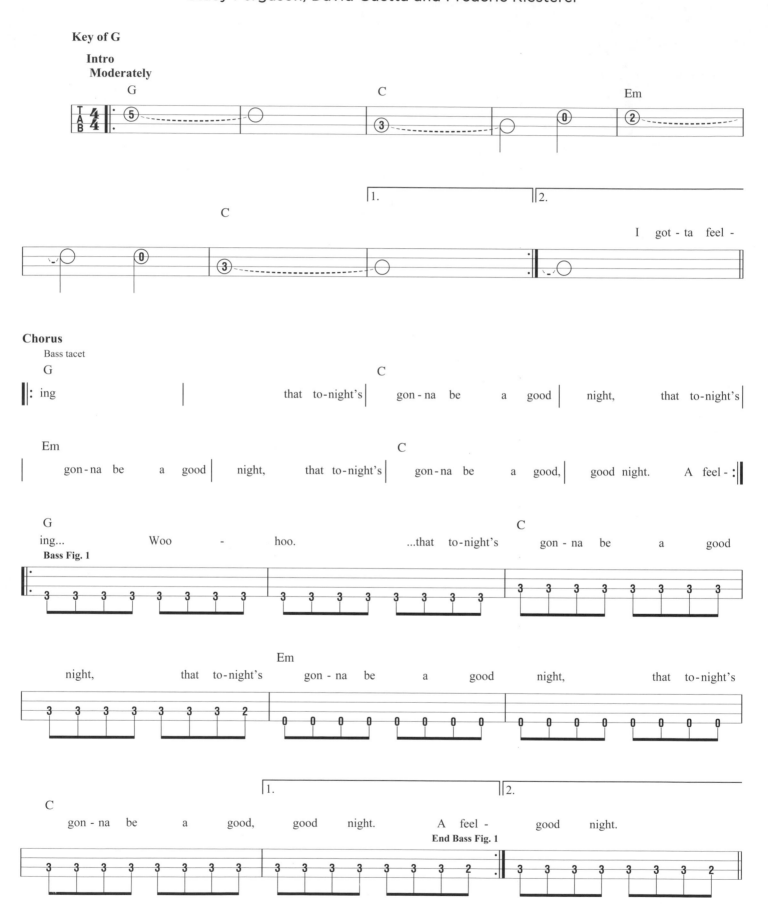

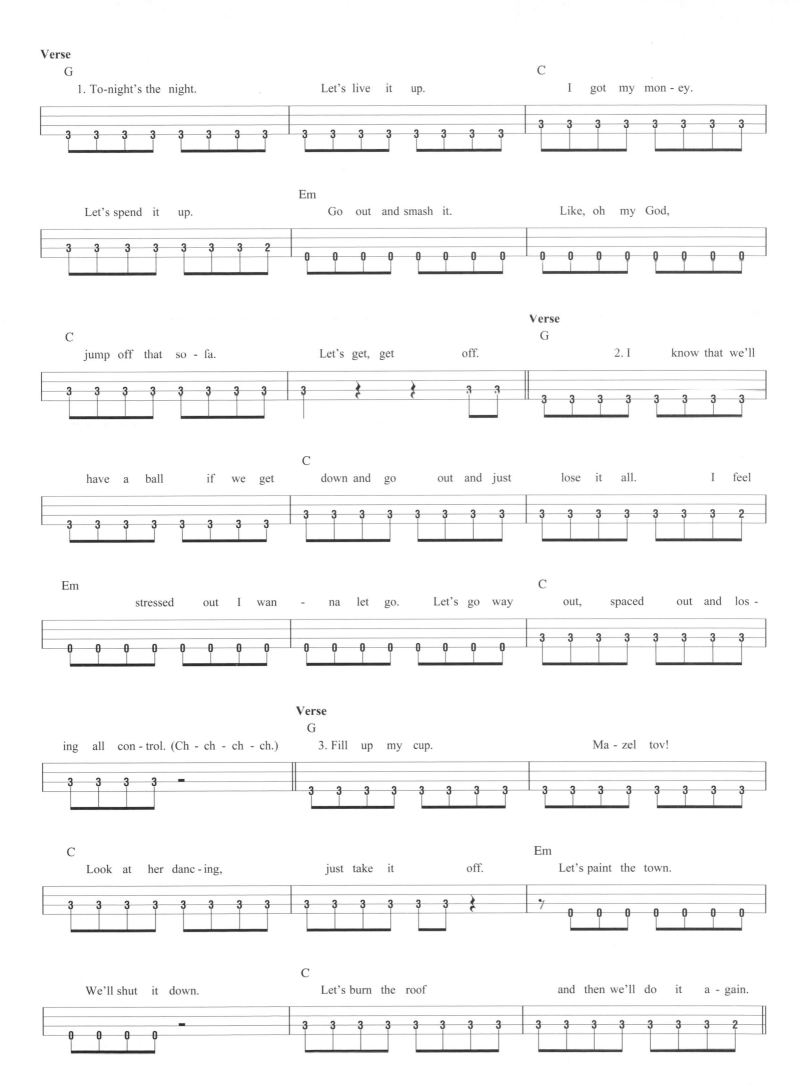

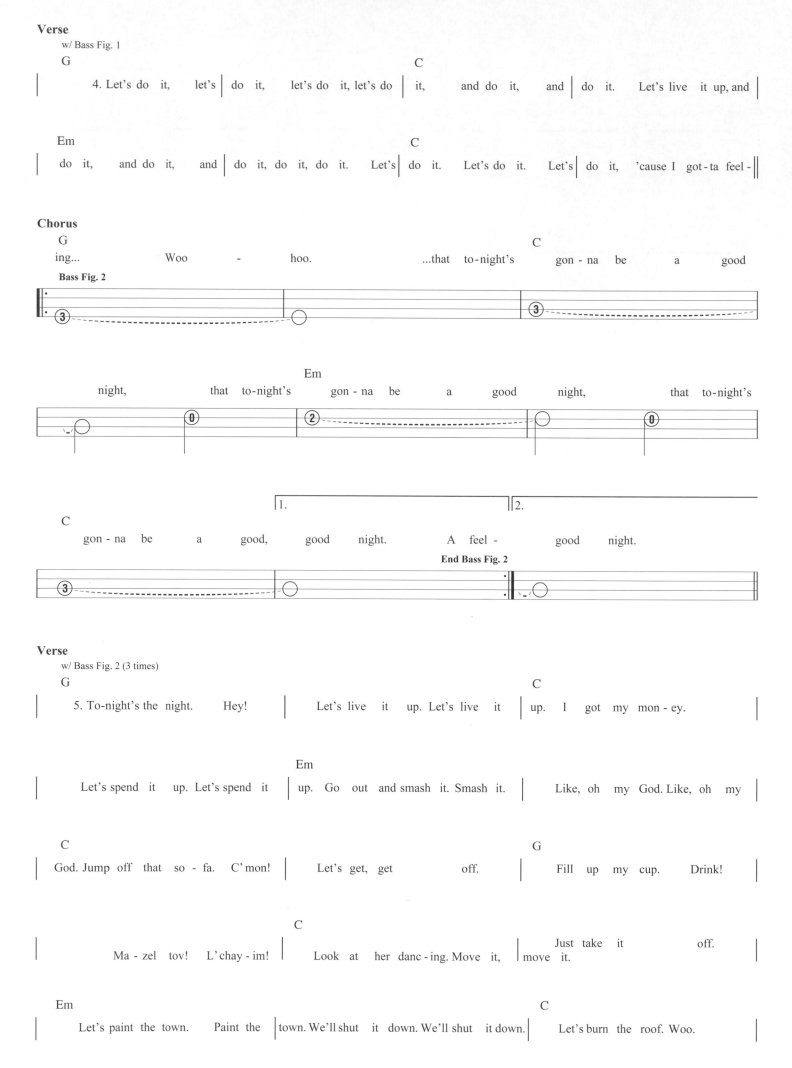

| G
| And then we'll do it a - gain. | Let's do it,   let's | do it,   let's do it, let's do |

C   Em
| it,   and do it,   and | do it.   Let's live it up, and | do it,   and do it,   and |

                                    C
| do it, do it, do it.   Let's | do it.   Let's do it.   Let's | do it, do it, do it, do it.   ‖

Verse
w/ Bass Fig. 1 (2 times)
  G   C
| 6. Here we come,   here we go. | We got - ta rock. | Eas - y come,   eas - y go. |

                                    Em
| Now we on top. | Feel the shot,   bod - y rock. | Rock it, don't stop. |

    C   G
| Round and round,   up and down, | a - round the clock. | Mon - day,   Tues - day, |

                                    C
| Wednes - day and Thurs - day. | Fri - day,   Sat - ur - day. | Sat - ur - day to Sun - day. |

  Em   C
| Get, get, get, get, get with us. | You know what we say,   say: | Par - ty ev - 'ry day. P - P - P - |

                    Outro-Chorus
                    w/ Bass Fig. 1 (2 times)
                      G
| Par - ty ev - 'ry day. And I'm feel - ‖: ing...   Woo   - | hoo.   ...that to-night's |

  C   Em
| gon - na be   a   good | night,   that to-night's | gon - na be   a   good |

                                                              ⌐1.
                                    C
| night,   that to-night's | gon - na be   a   good, | good   night.   A feel - :‖

⌐2.
                                    G
| good   night. | Woo   - | hoo. |

I Love Rock 'N Roll

Words and Music by Alan Merrill and Jake Hooker

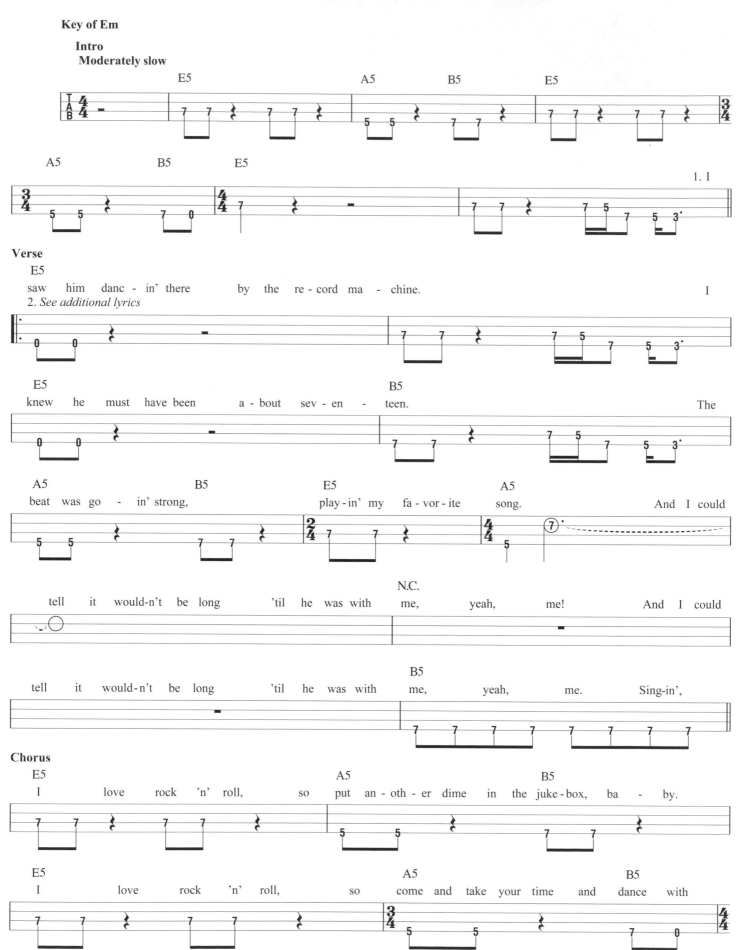

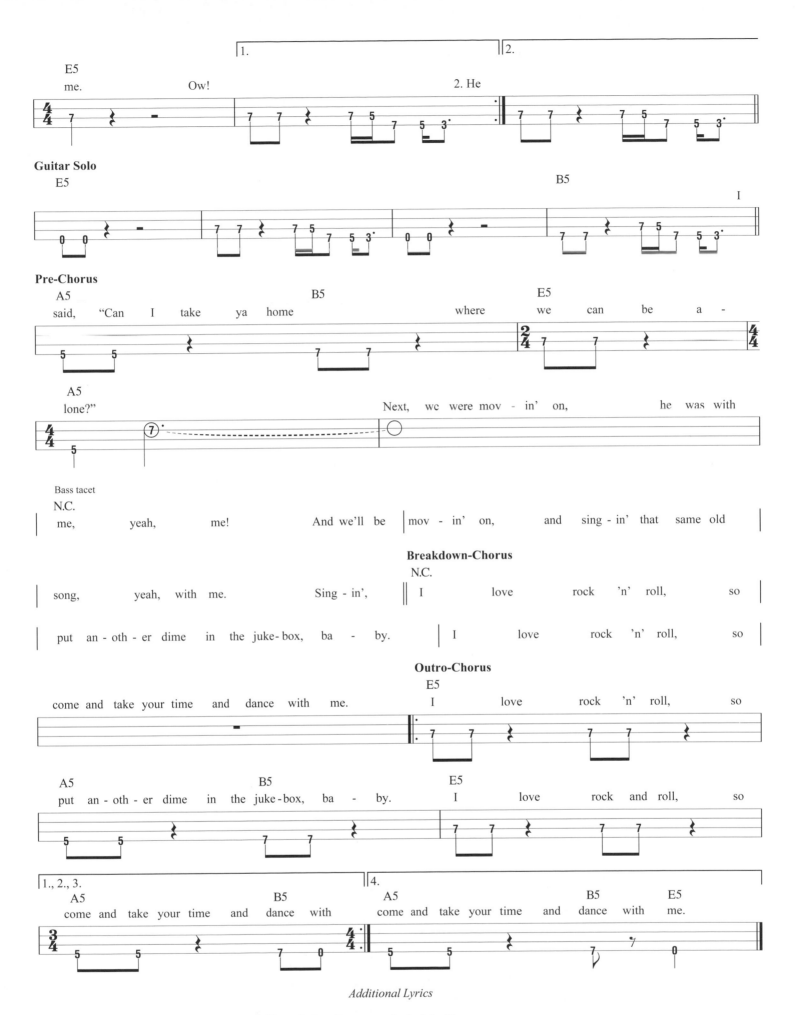

Additional Lyrics

2. He smiled, so I got up and asked for his name.
    "That don't matter," he said, "'cause it's all the same."
    I said, "Can I take ya home where we can be alone?"
    And next, we were movin' on, he was with me, yeah, me.
    Next, we were movin' on, he was with me, yeah, me, singin',...

The Lemon Song

Words and Music by Chester Burnett, John Bonham, Jimmy Page, Robert Plant and John Paul Jones

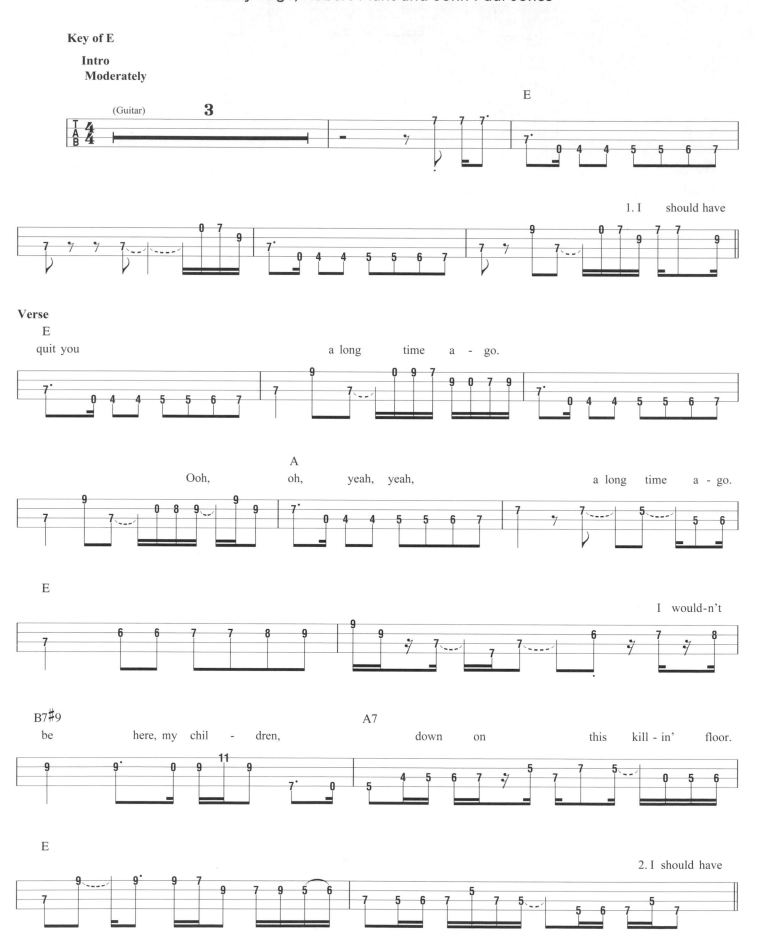

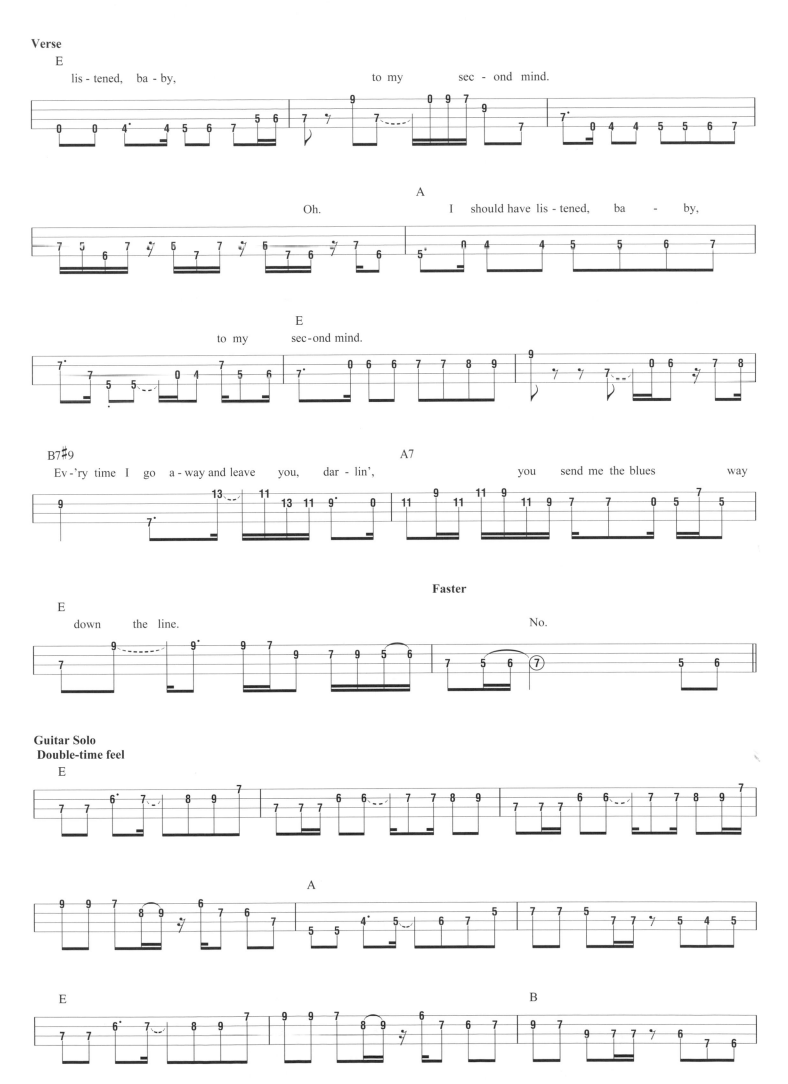

53

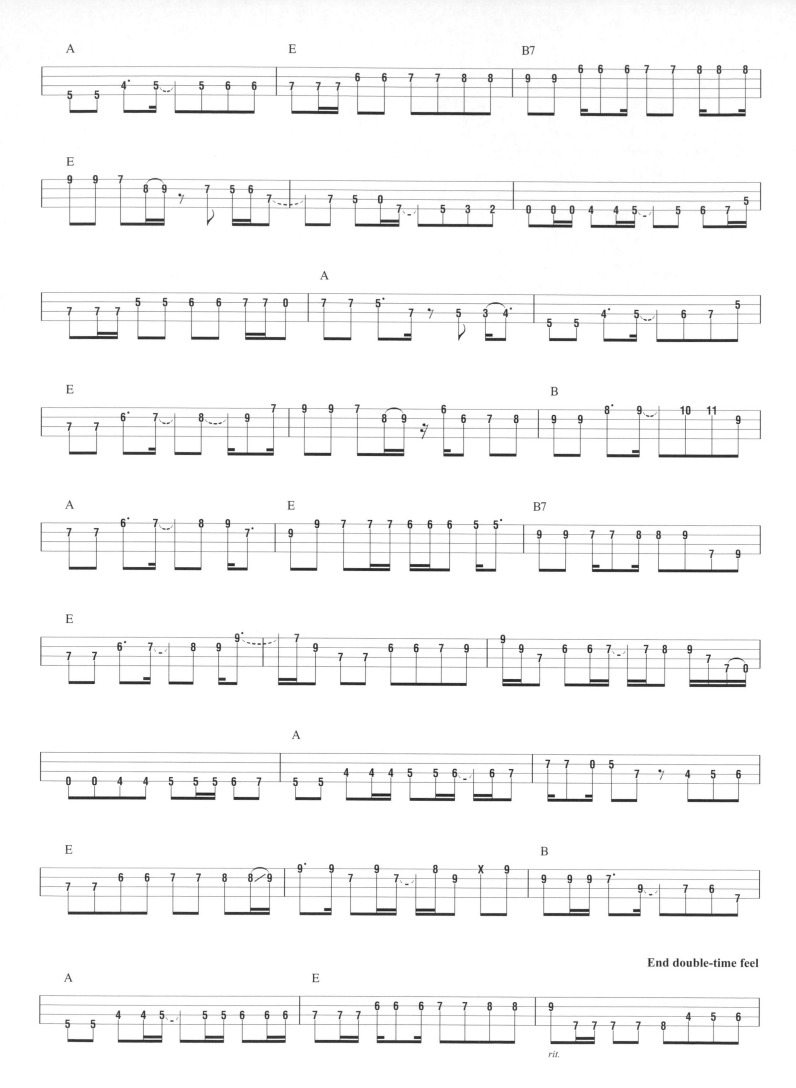

End double-time feel

rit.

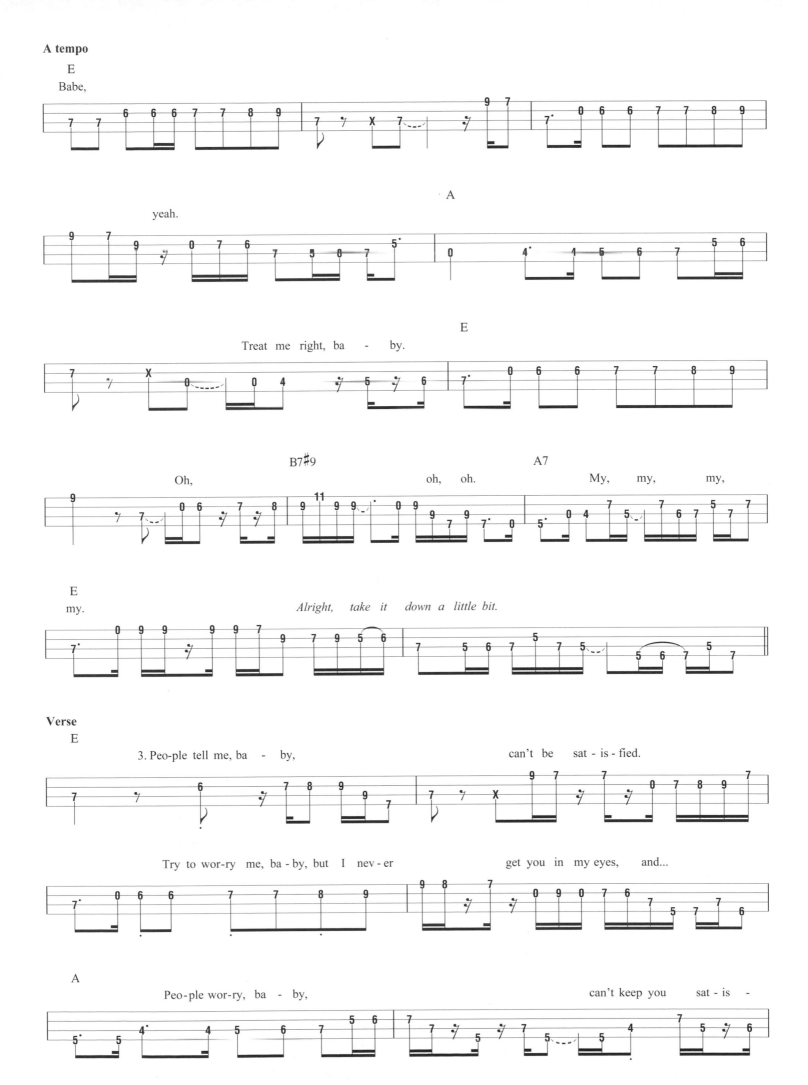

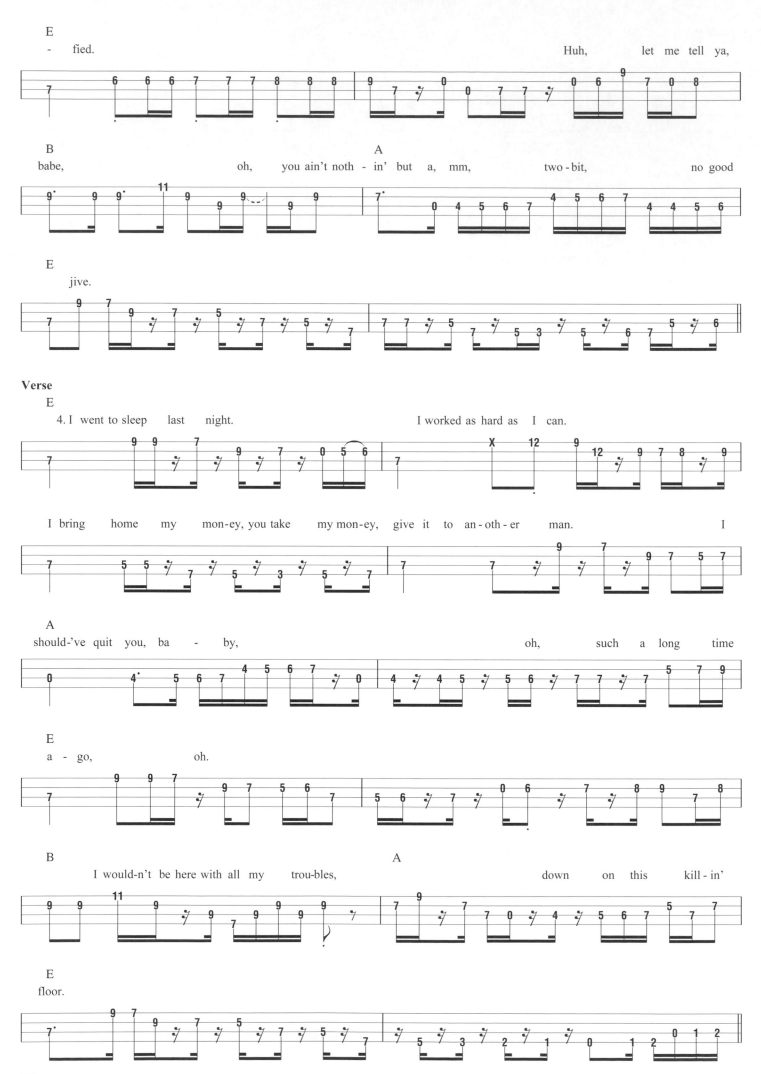

56

Verse

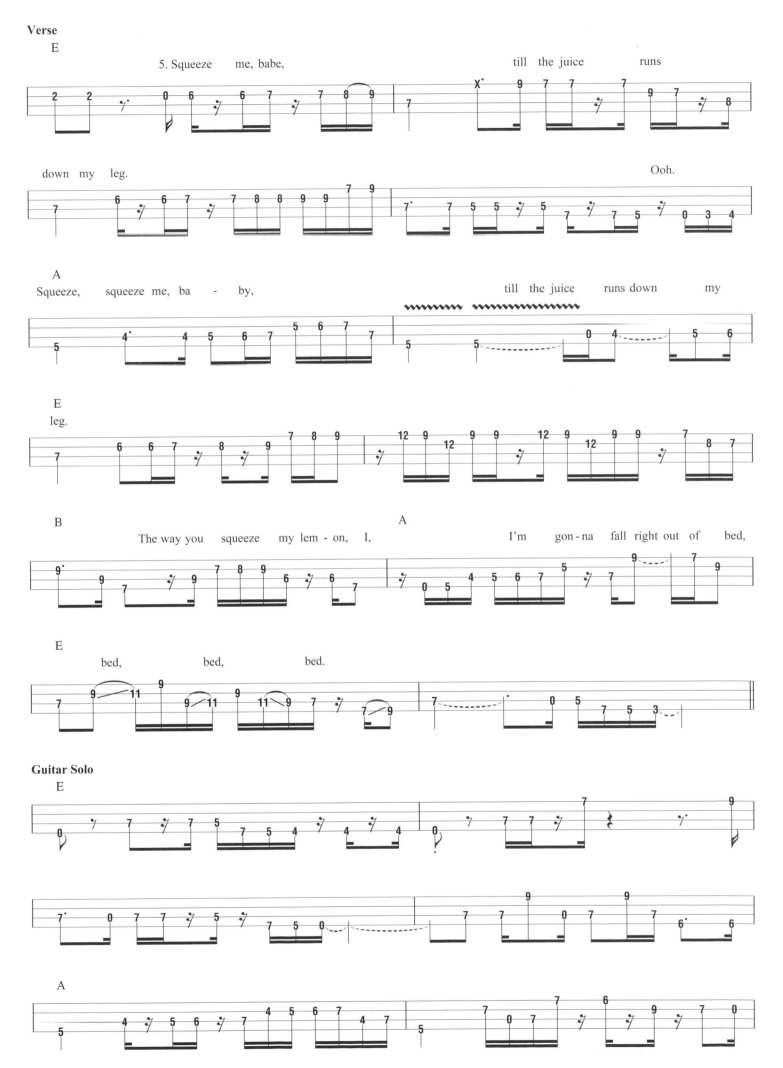

Guitar Solo
Double-time feel

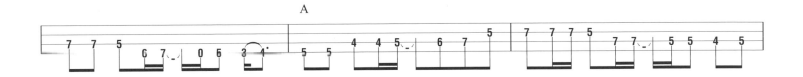

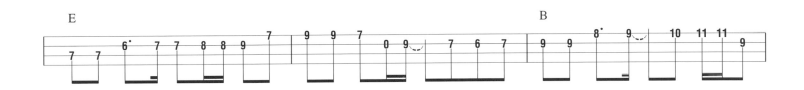

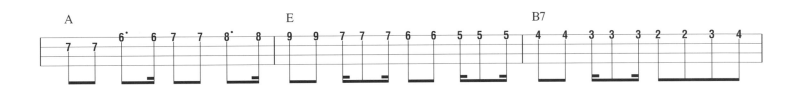

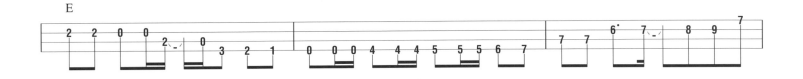

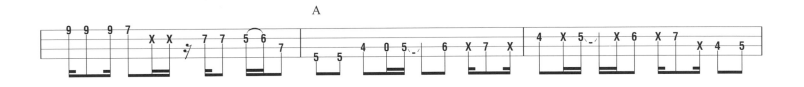

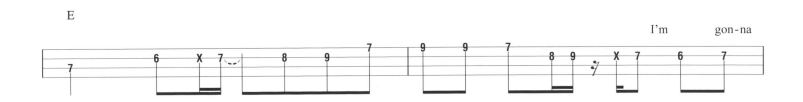

I'm gon-na

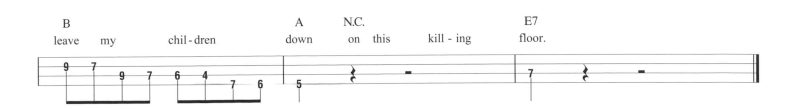

leave my chil-dren   down on this kill-ing floor.

Like a Stone

Lyrics by Chris Cornell
Music written and arranged by Audioslave

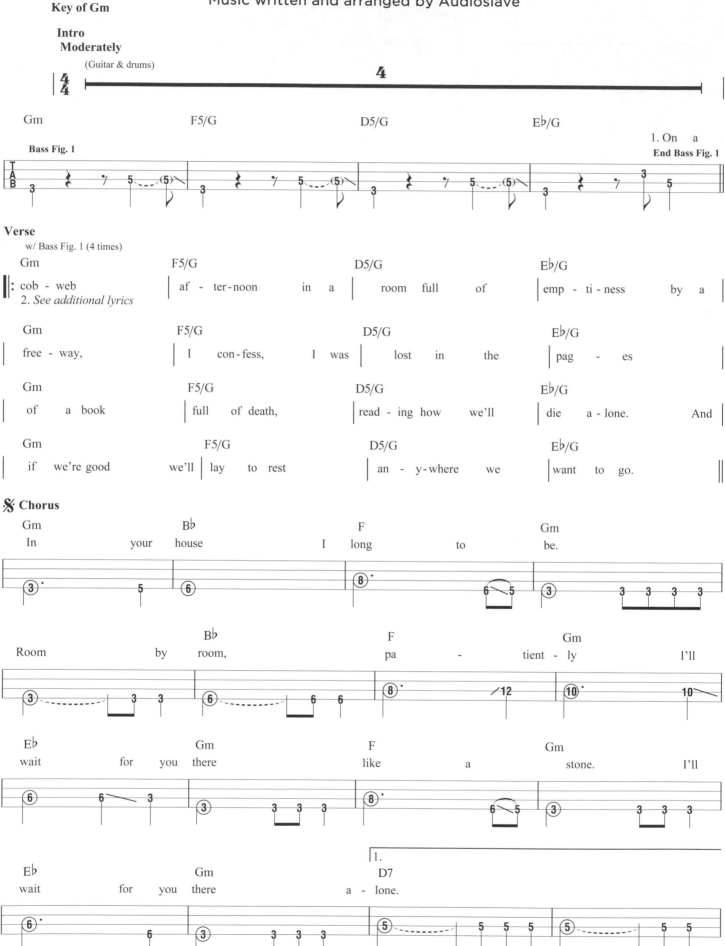

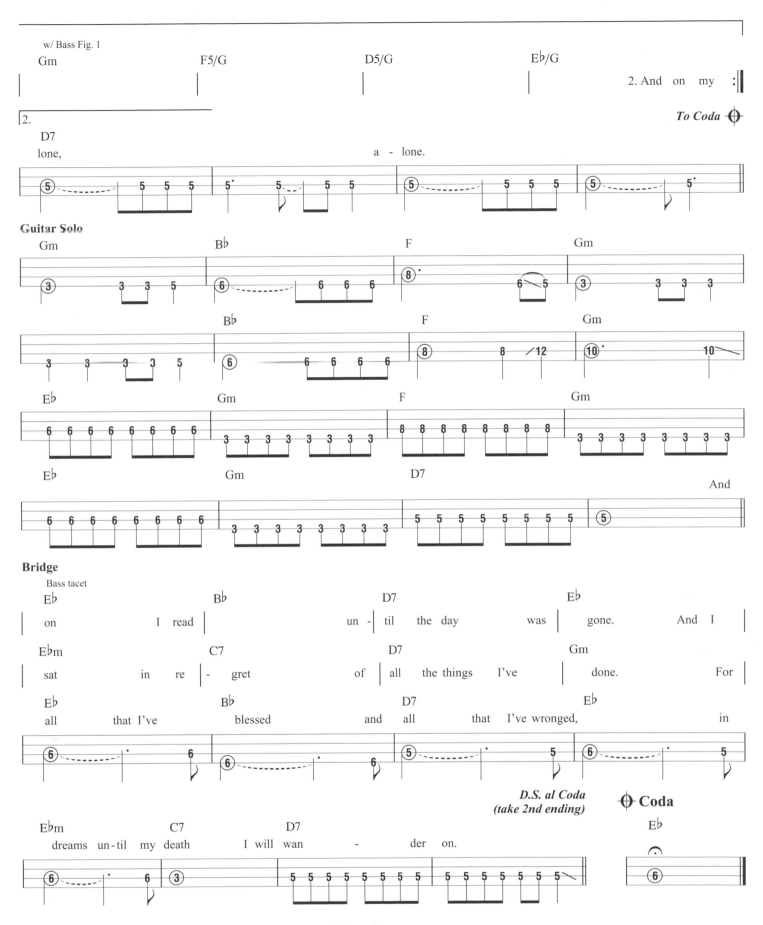

Additional Lyrics

2. And on my deathbed I will pray
   To the gods and the angels
   Like a pagan to anyone
   Who will take me to heaven.
   To a place I recall,
   I was there so long ago.
   The sky was bruised, the wine was bled,
   And there you led me on.

Living After Midnight

Words and Music by Glenn Raymond Tipton, Robert Halford and Kenneth Downing

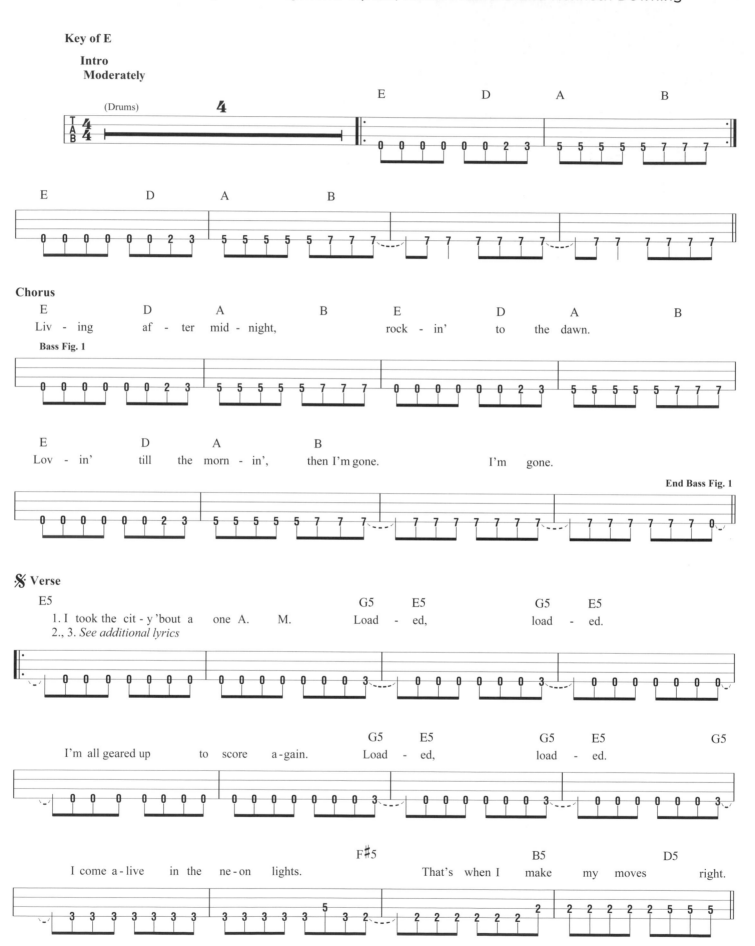

Chorus

1st & 3rd times, w/ Bass Fig. 1
2nd time, w/ Bass Fig. 1 (1st 7 meas.)

E	D	A	B	E	D	A	B
Liv - ing	af - ter	mid - night,		rock - in'	to the	dawn.	

1.

To Coda ⊕

E	D	A	B
Lov - in'	till the	morn - in',	then I'm gone,	I'm gone.

2.

Bridge

A	D/A	A	D/A	A	E5	G5	E5	A
				I'm		aim - in'	for	ya.

Bass Fig. 2   End Bass Fig. 2

```
7 7 7 7 7 7 5 | 5 5 5 5 5 5 5 | 5 5 5 5 5 5 5 0 | 0 0 0 0 0 3 | 0 0 0 0 0 5
```

w/ Bass Fig. 2 (2 times)

D/A	A	D/A	A	E5	G5	E5	A
				I'm	gon	- na floor	ya.

D/A	A	D/A	A	E5	G5	E5	A
				My	bod	- y's com - ing	

D/A	A	D/A	A	B5	D5	B5
				all	night	long!

```
5 5 5 5 5 5 5 | 5 5 5 5 5 5 7 | 7 7 7 7 7 7 | 7 7 7 7 7 5 3
```

Guitar Solo
w/ Bass Fig. 1

D.S. al Coda

8

⊕ Coda

Outro-Chorus
w/ Bass Fig. 1 (till fade)

E	D	A	B	E	D
:Liv - ing	af - ter	mid - night,		rock - in'	to the

Repeat and fade

A	B	E	D	A	B
dawn.	Lov - in'	till the	morn - in',	then I'm gone,	I'm gone.

Additional Lyrics

2. Got gleamin' chrome reflecting feel.
   Loaded, loaded.
   Ready to take on ev'ry deal.
   Loaded, loaded.
   My pulse is racin', hot to take.
   But this motor's revved up, fit to break.

3. The air's electric, sparkin' power.
   Loaded, loaded.
   I'm gettin' harder by the hour.
   Loaded, loaded.
   I set my sights and then home in.
   The joint starts fly'n' when I begin.

Mony, Mony

Words and Music by Bobby Bloom, Tommy James, Ritchie Cordell and Bo Gentry

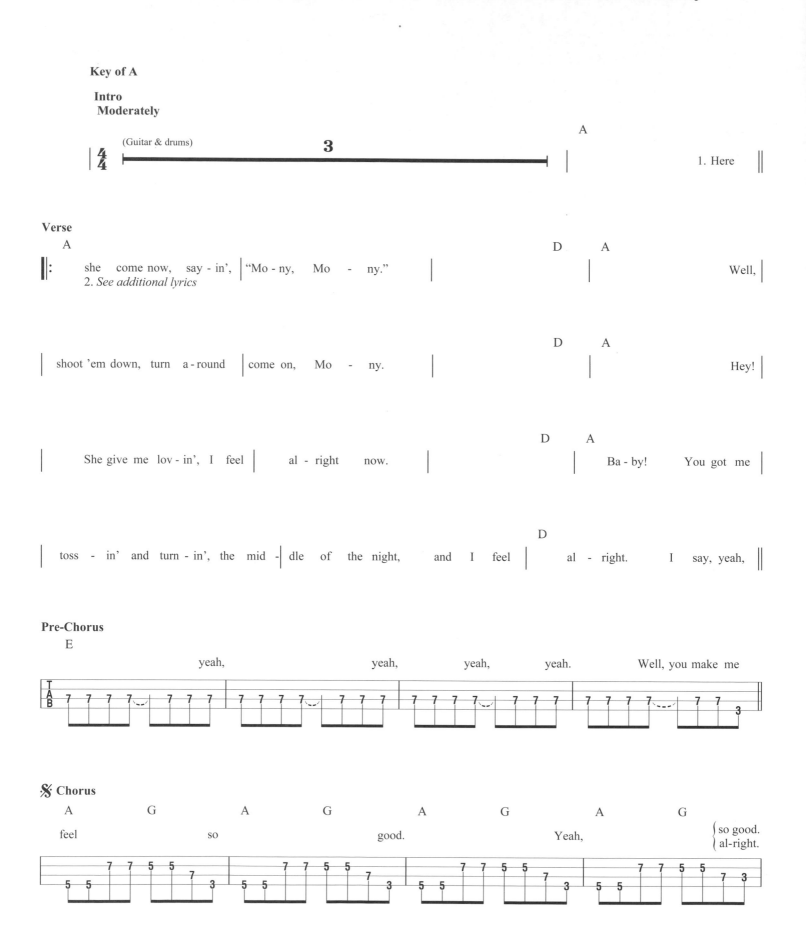

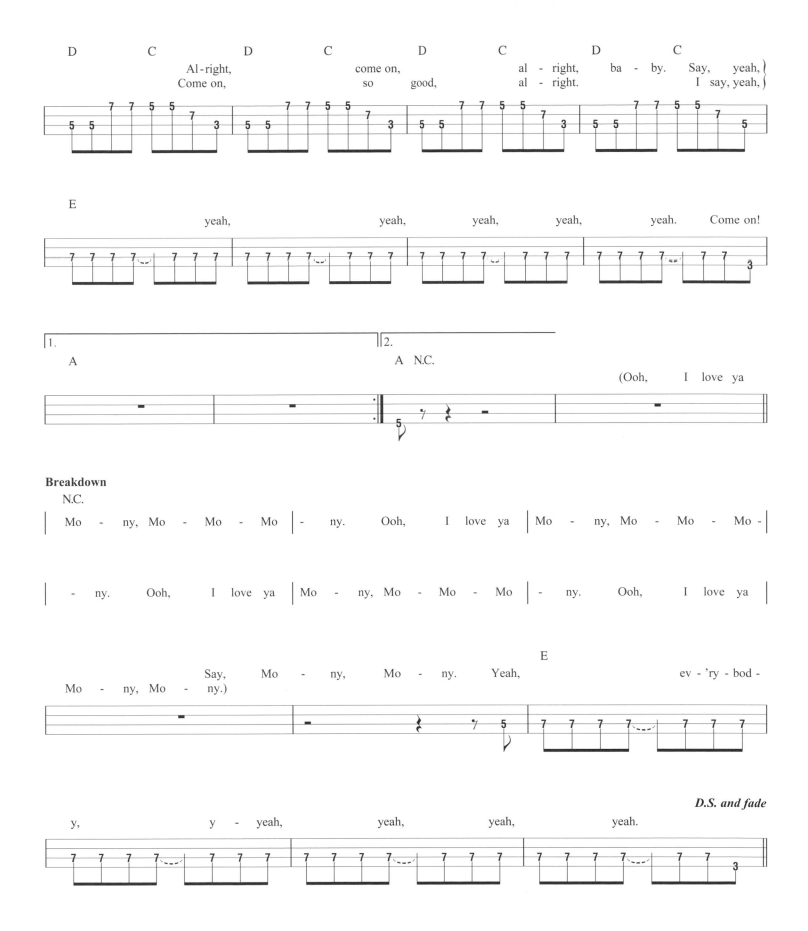

Additional Lyrics

2. Wake me, shake me, Mony, Mony.
   Shotgun, get it done. Come on, Mony.
   Don't 'cha stop cookin', it feels so good, yeah.
   Hey! Well, but don't stop now, hey,
   Come on, Mony. Well, come on, Mony.

My Own Worst Enemy

Words and Music by Jeremy Popoff, Jay Popoff, Kevin Baldes and Allen Shellenberger

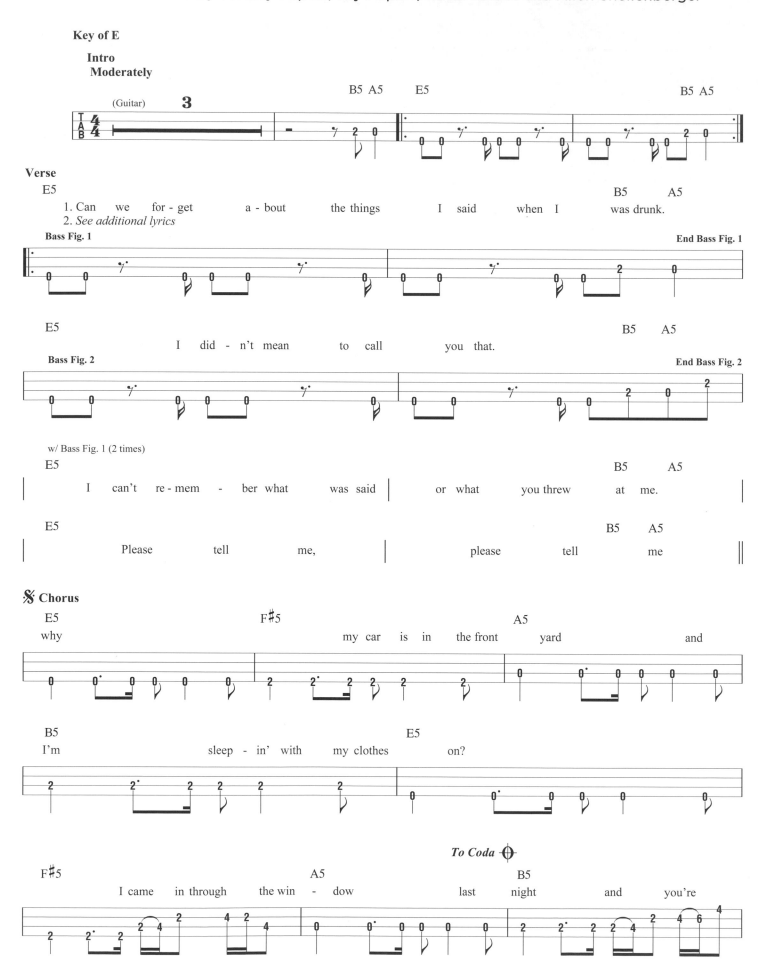

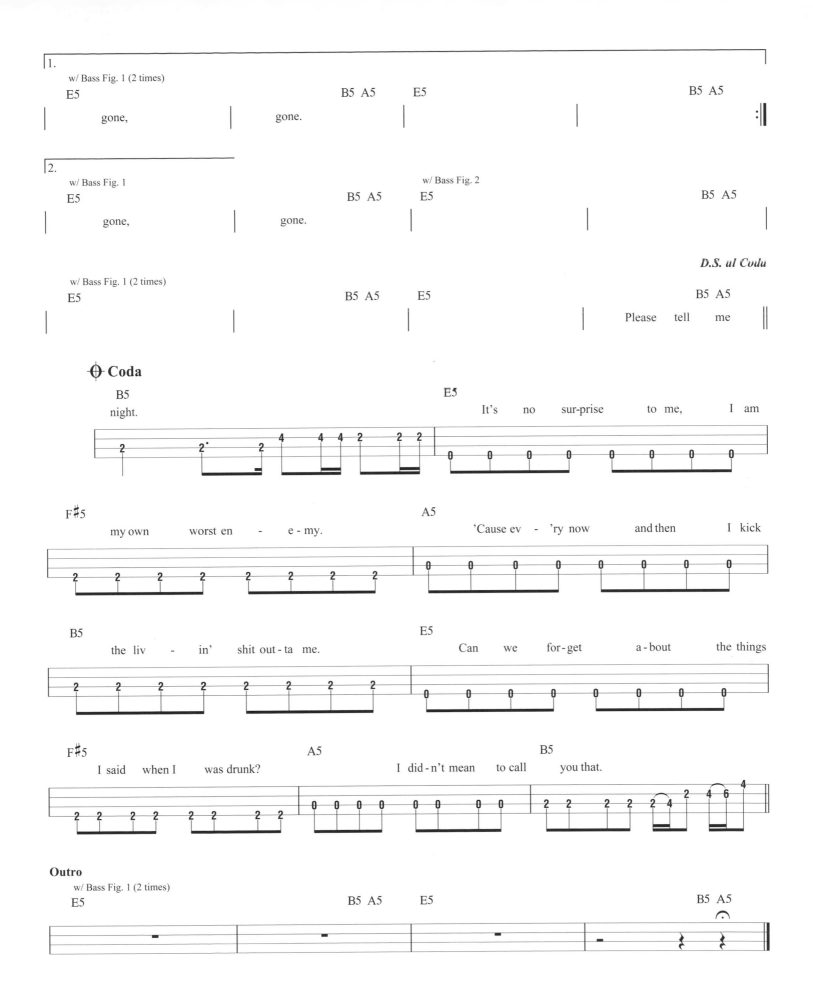

Additional Lyrics

2. It's no surprise to me, I am my own worst enemy.
   'Cause ev'ry now and then I kick the livin' shit outta me.
   The smoke alarm is goin' off and there's a cigarette
   Still burnin'. Please tell me…

Nothing Else Matters

Words and Music by James Hetfield and Lars Ulrich

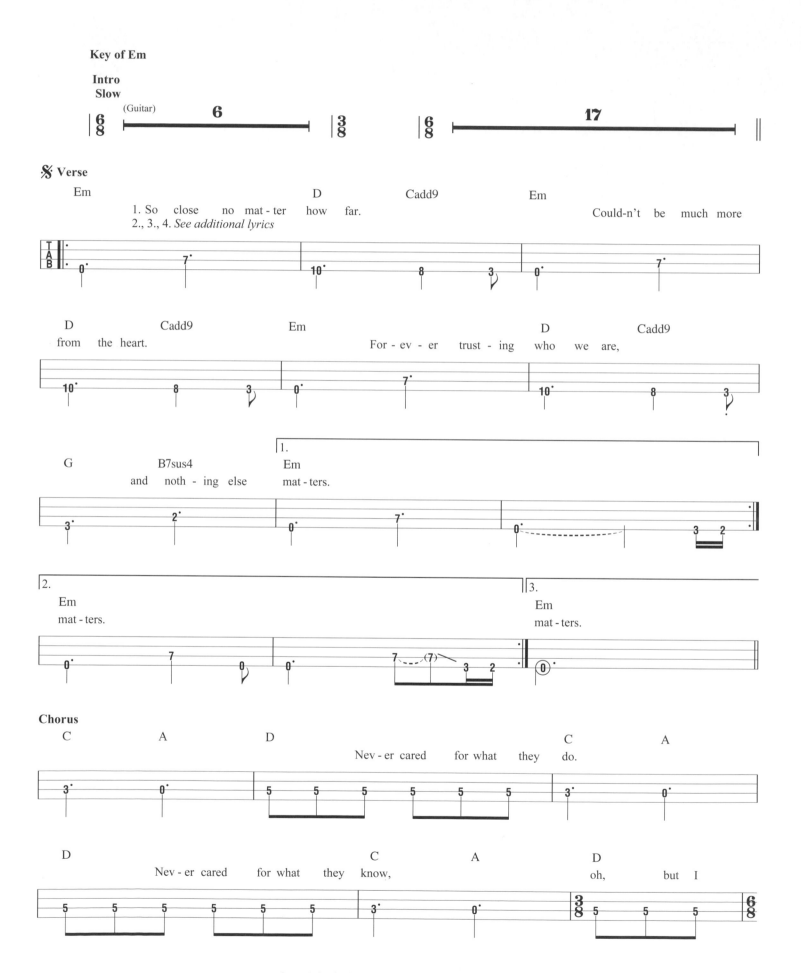

w/ Bass Fig. 1 (3 times)

Outro

Repeat and fade

Additional Lyrics

2. Never opened myself this way.
Life is ours, we live it our way.
All these words I don't just say,
And nothing else matters.

3., 6. Trust I seek and I find in you.
Ev'ry day for us, something new.
Open mind for a diff'rent view,
And nothing else matters.

4. So close no matter how far.
It couldn't be much more from the heart.
Forever trusting who we are,
And nothing else matters.

Old Time Rock & Roll

Words and Music by George Jackson and Thomas E. Jones III

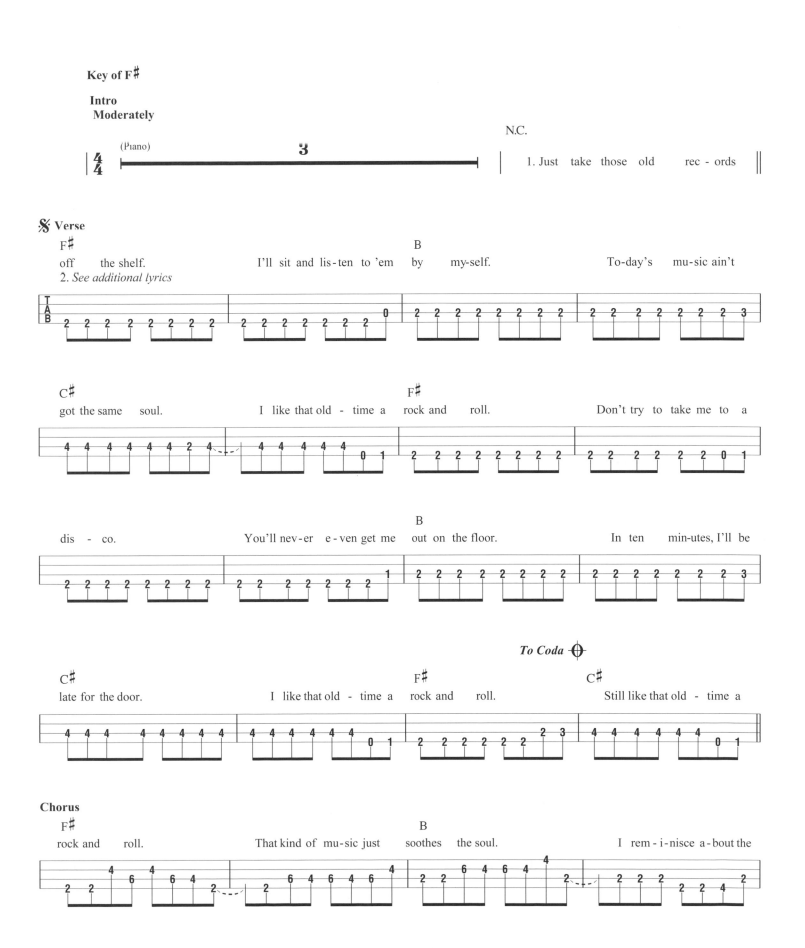

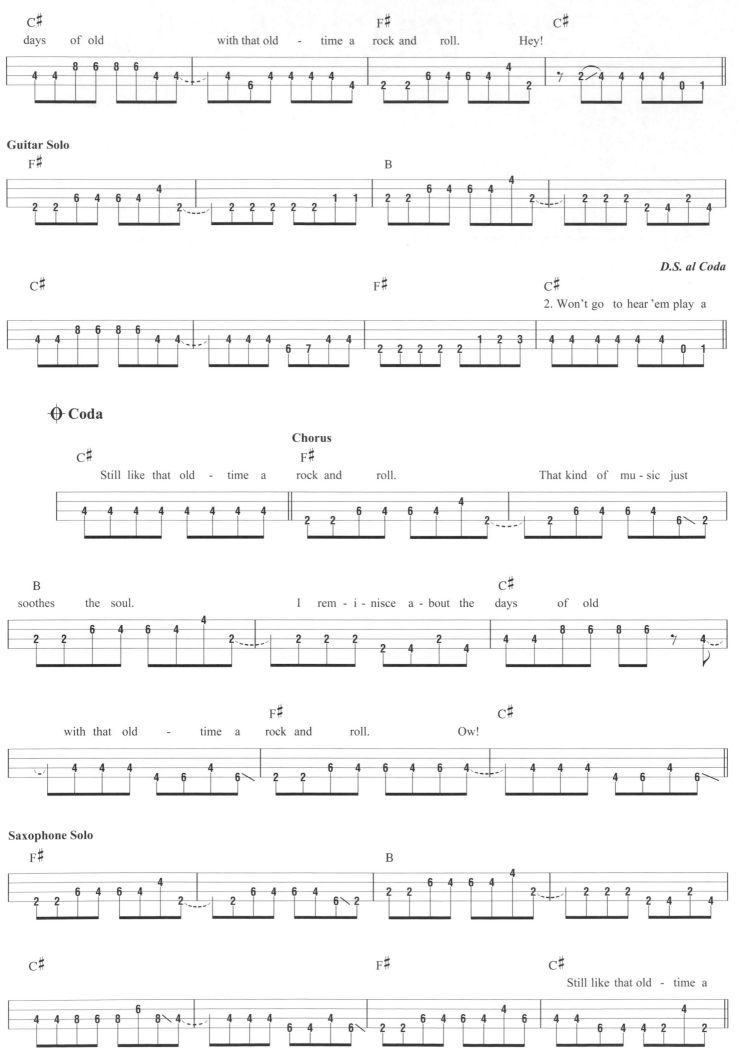

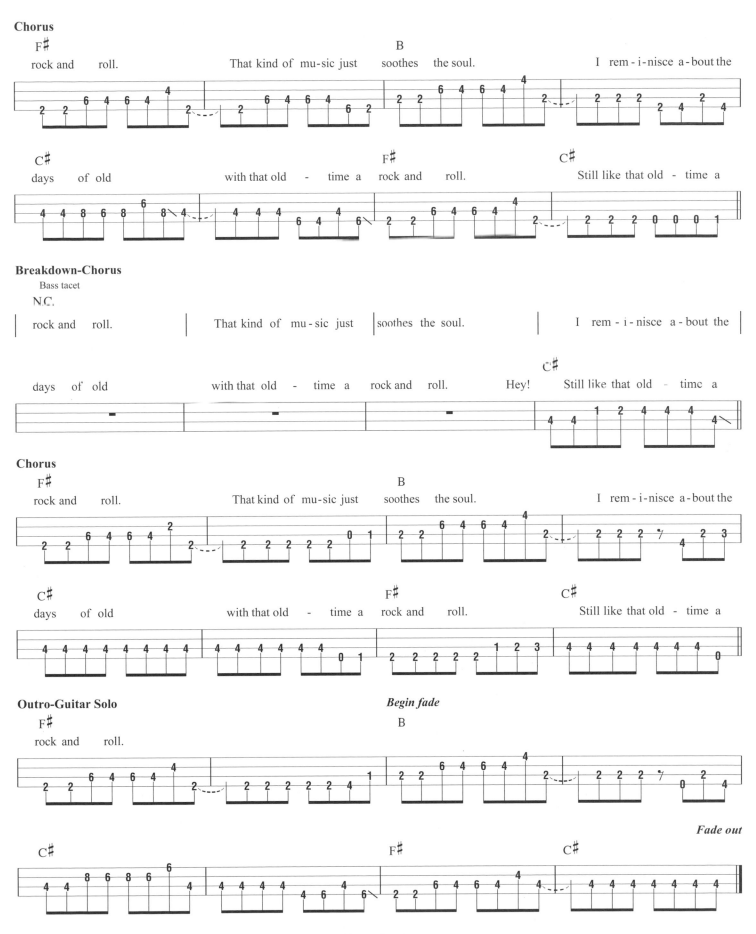

Additional Lyrics

2. Won't go to hear 'em play a tango.
   I'd rather hear some blues or funky old soul.
   There's only one sure way to get me to go:
   Start playing old time rock and roll.
   Call me a relic, call me what you will.
   Say I'm old-fashioned, say I'm over the hill.
   Today's music ain't got the same soul.
   I like that old time rock and roll.

Pour Some Sugar on Me

Words and Music by Joe Elliott, Phil Collen, Richard Savage,
Richard Allen, Steve Clark and R.J. Lange

Key of C♯m

Intro
Moderately
N.C.

Step in - side.   (Walk this way.)   You and me, babe.   Hey, hey!

C♯5   N.C.

Verse
Bass tacet
N.C.

1. Love is like a bomb, ba - by, come and get it on.   Liv - ing like a lov - er with a ra - dar phone.

Look - in' like a tramp, like a vid - e - o vamp.   Dem - o - li - tion wom - an, can I be your man?

C♯5

(Hey!)   Hey!)

Raz - zle and a daz - zle and a flash a lit - tle light.   Tel - e - vi - sion lov - er, ba - by, go all night.

Some - time, an - y - time, sug - ar me sweet.   Lit - tle miss in - no - cent, sug - ar me. Yeah.

Yeah.   Come on.

Pre-Chorus
F♯5 C♯5 B5   F♯5 C♯5 B5   E5 B5 A5
Take the bot - tle,   shake it up.   Break the bub - ble,

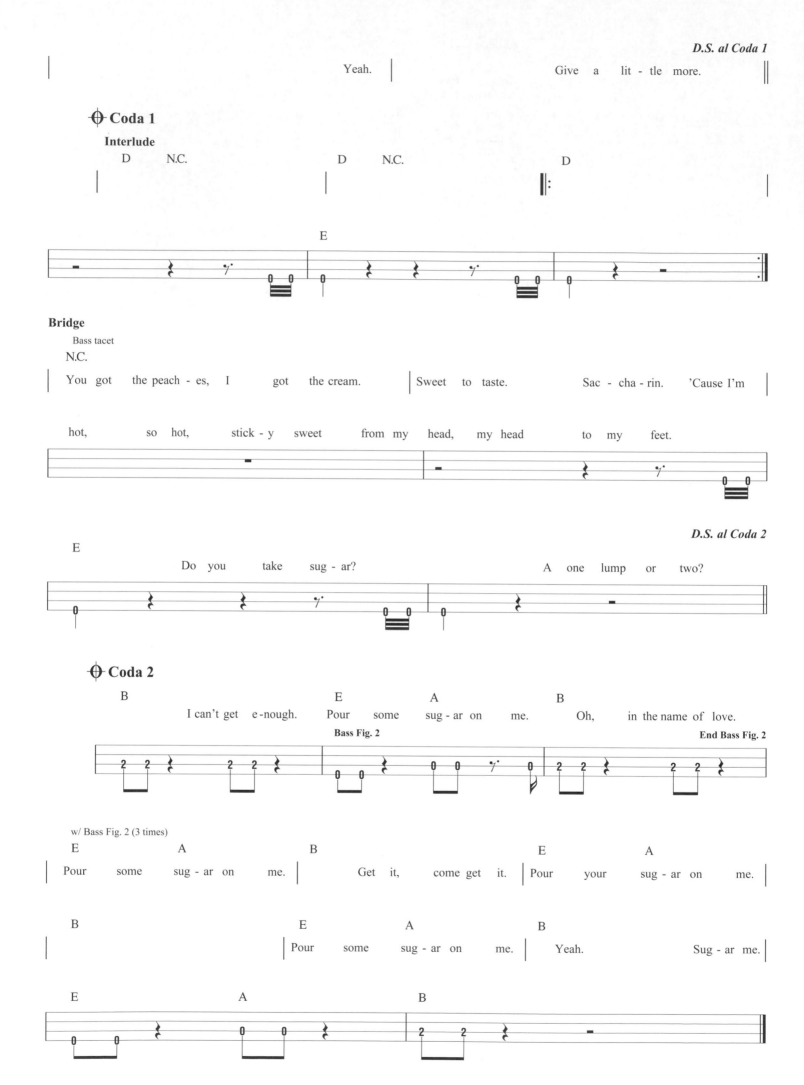

Yeah.   Give a lit - tle more.

Coda 1

Interlude

Bridge

Bass tacet

N.C.

You got the peach - es, I got the cream.   Sweet to taste.   Sac - cha - rin.   'Cause I'm

hot,   so hot,   stick - y sweet   from my   head,   my head   to my   feet.

D.S. al Coda 2

Do you   take sug - ar?   A one lump or two?

Coda 2

I can't get e -nough.   Pour some sug - ar on me.   Oh,   in the name of love.

Bass Fig. 2   **End Bass Fig. 2**

w/ Bass Fig. 2 (3 times)

Pour   some sug - ar on   me.   Get it,   come get it.   Pour your   sug - ar on   me.

Pour   some   sug - ar on   me.   Yeah.   Sug - ar me.

Say It Ain't So

Words and Music by Rivers Cuomo

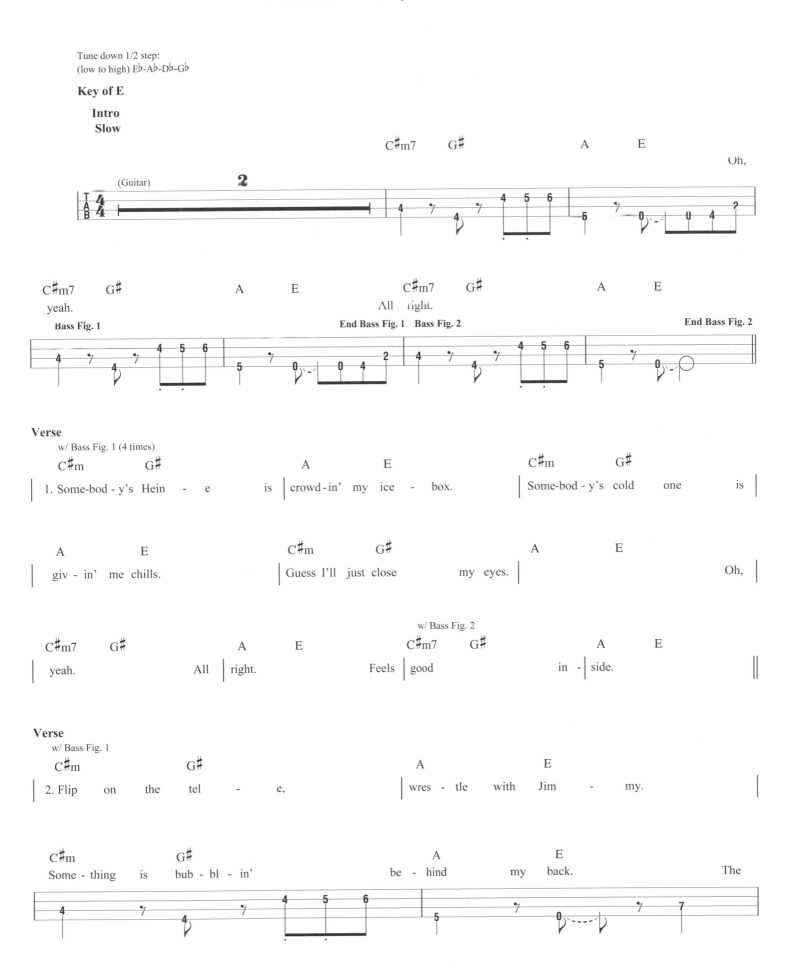

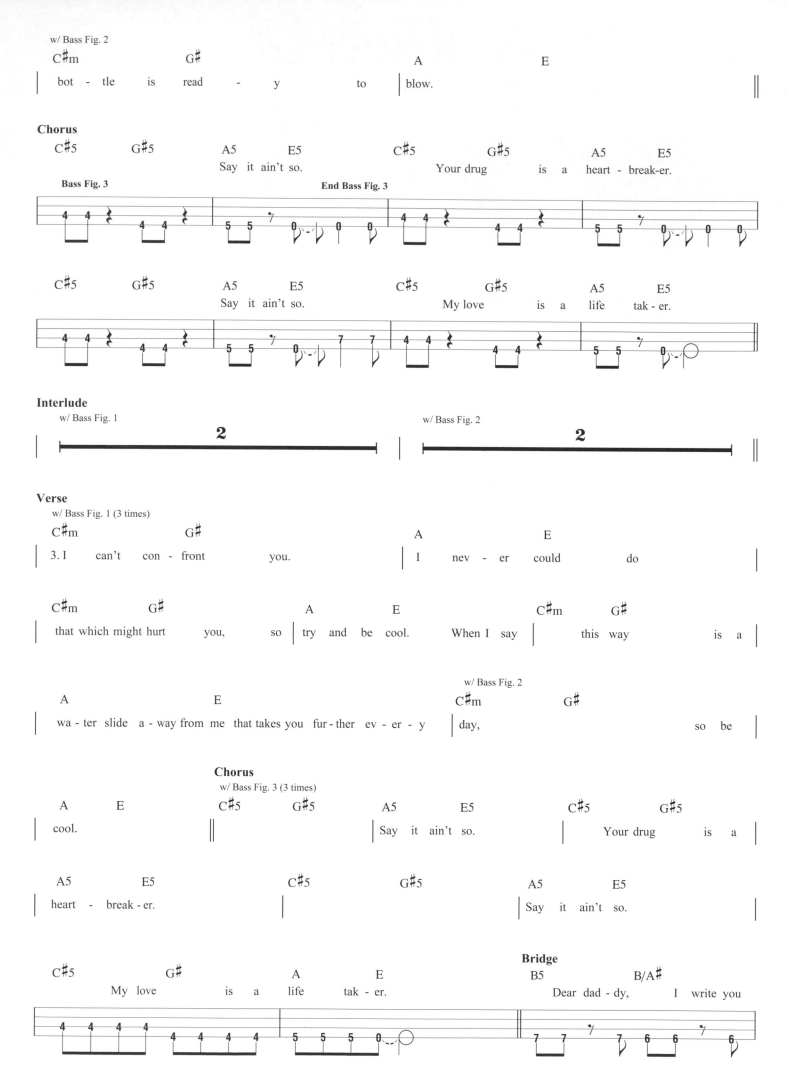

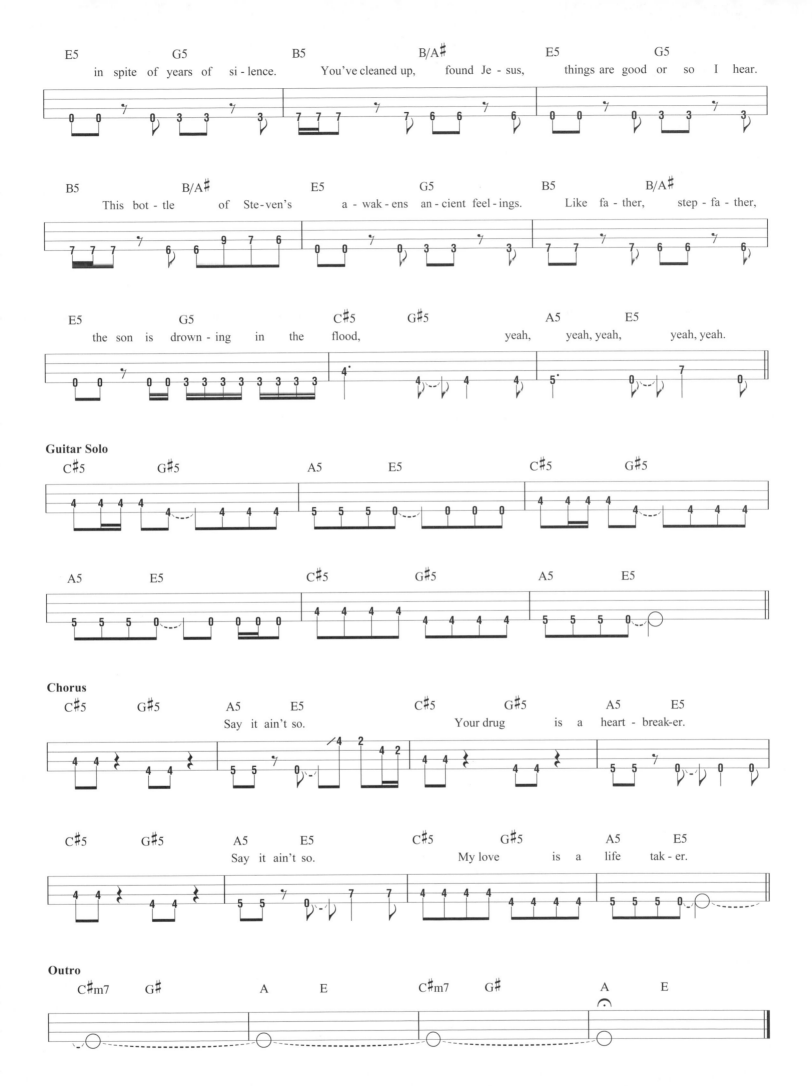

Runnin' with the Devil

Words and Music by Edward Van Halen, Alex Van Halen, Michael Anthony and David Lee Roth

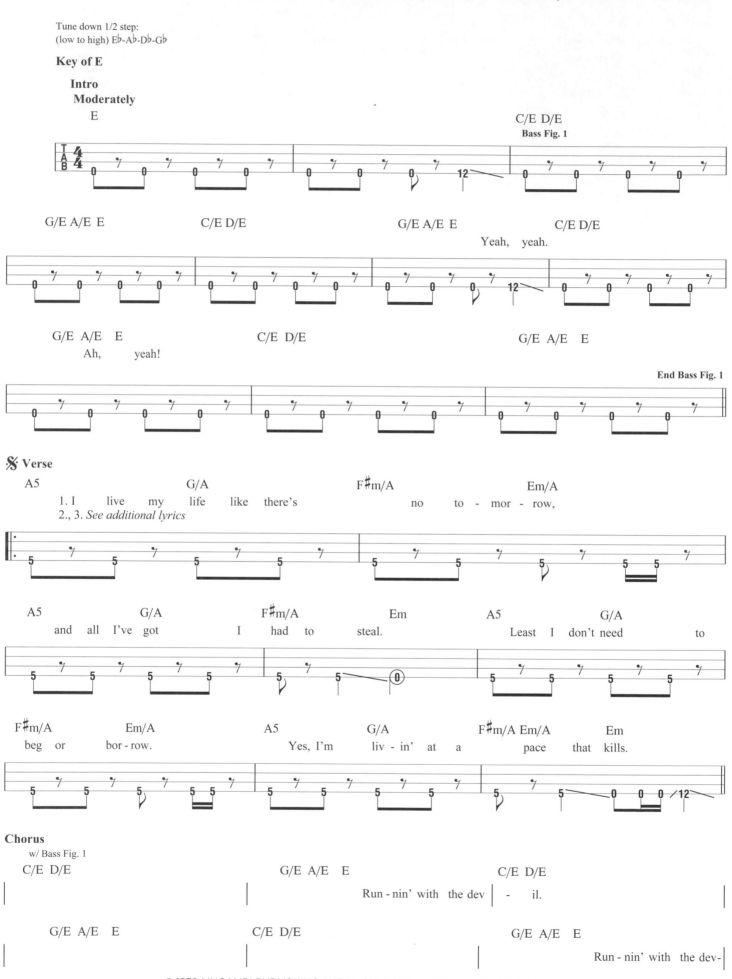

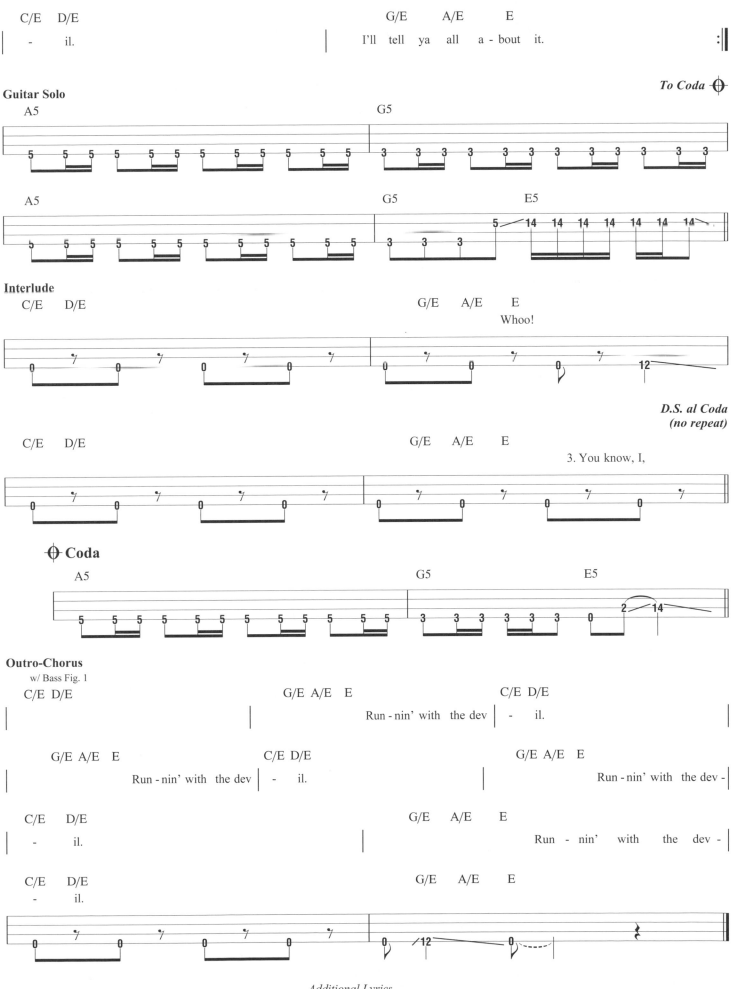

Seven Nation Army
Words and Music by Jack White

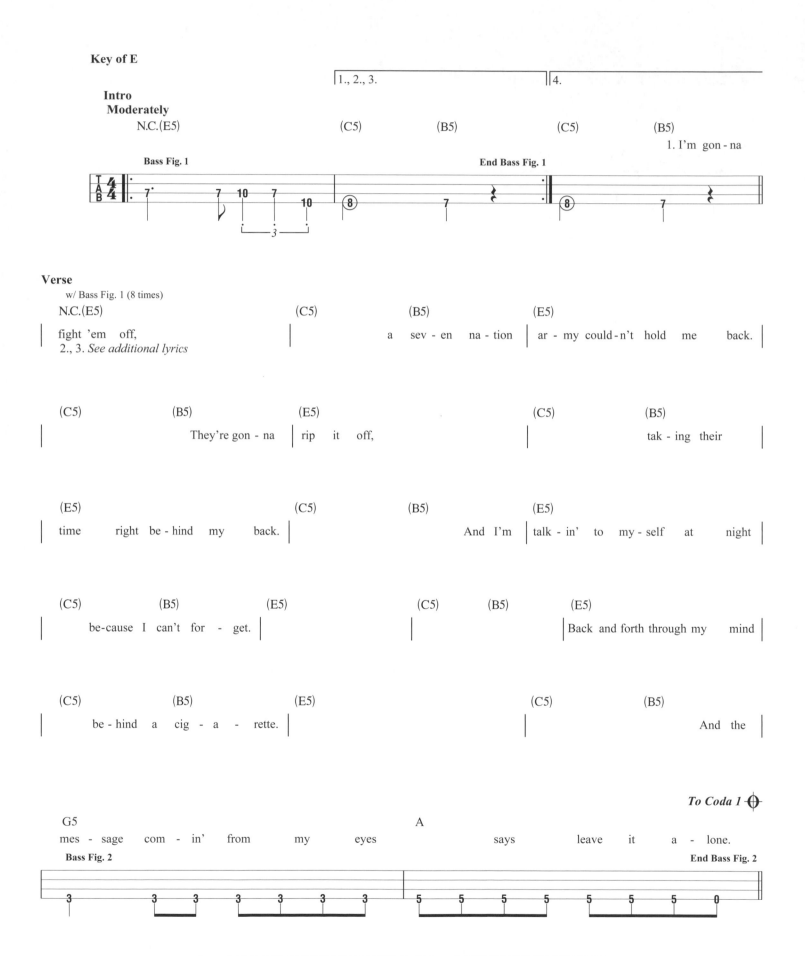

Interlude

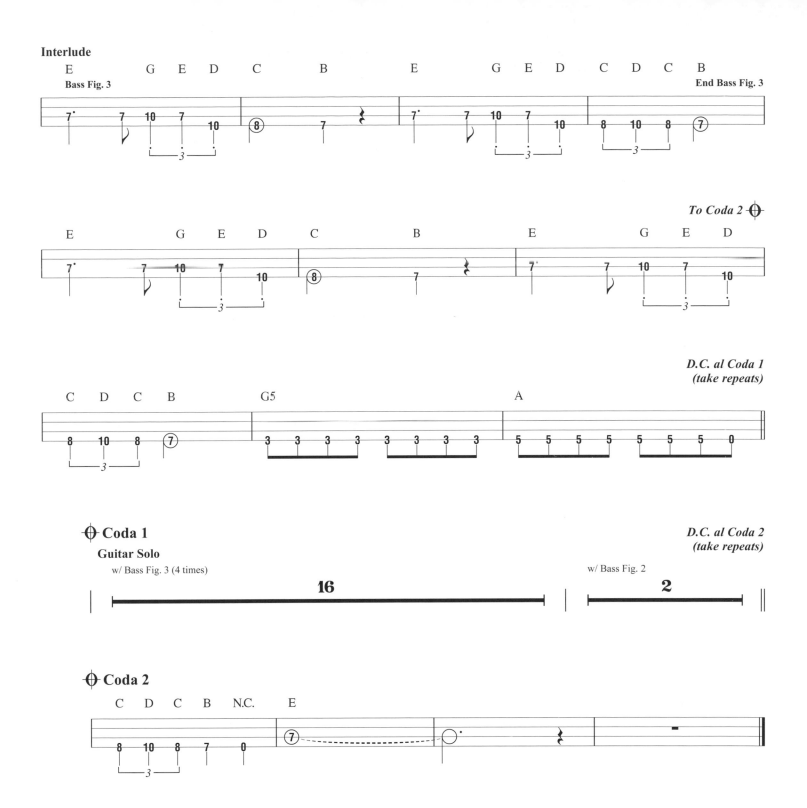

To Coda 2 ⊕

D.C. al Coda 1
(take repeats)

⊕ **Coda 1**

Guitar Solo

w/ Bass Fig. 3 (4 times)

16

D.C. al Coda 2
(take repeats)

w/ Bass Fig. 2

2

⊕ **Coda 2**

Additional Lyrics

2. Don't wanna hear about it, ev'ry single one's got a story to tell.
   Ev'ryone knows about it, from the Queen of England to the hounds of hell.
   And if I catch it coming back my way, I'm gonna serve it to you.
   And that ain't what you want to hear, but that's what I'll do.
   And the feeling coming from my bones says find a home.

3. I'm goin' to Wichita, far from this opera forevermore.
   I'm gonna work the straw, make the sweat drip out of every pore.
   And I'm bleeding, and I'm bleeding, and I'm bleeding right before the Lord.
   All the words are gonna bleed from me and I will think no more.
   And the stains coming from my blood tell me go back home.

Sharp Dressed Man

Words and Music by Billy F Gibbons, Dusty Hill and Frank Lee Beard

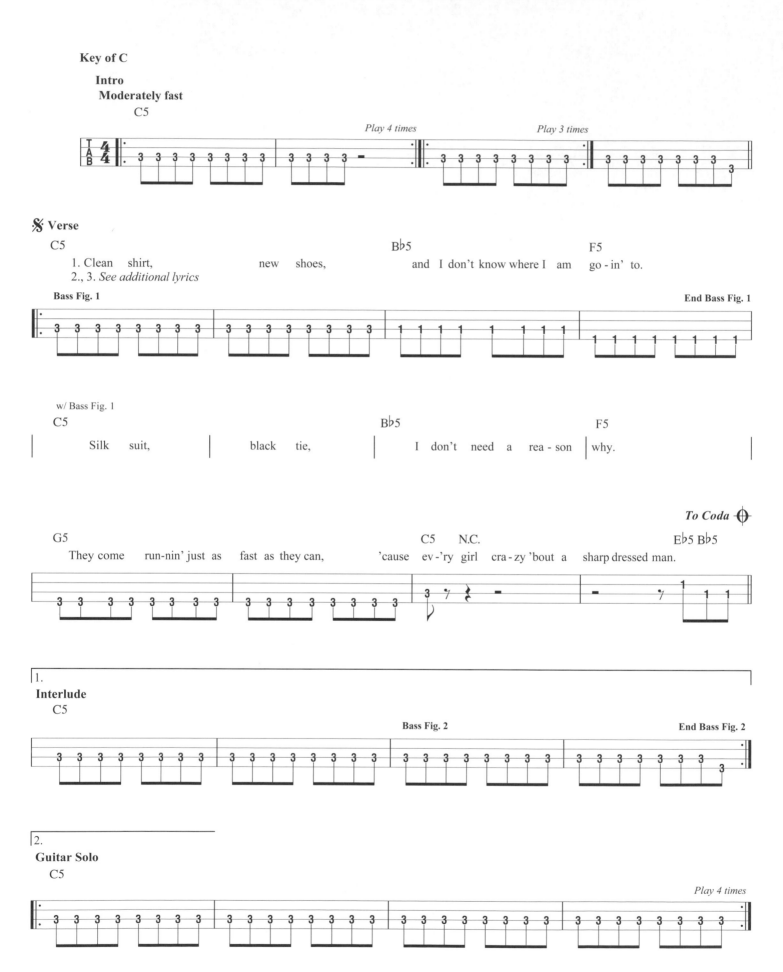

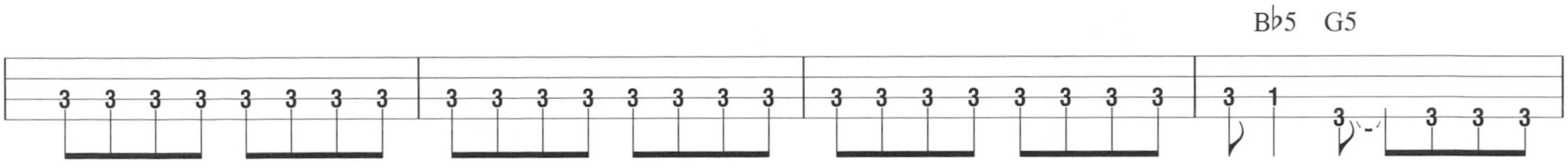
B♭5 G5

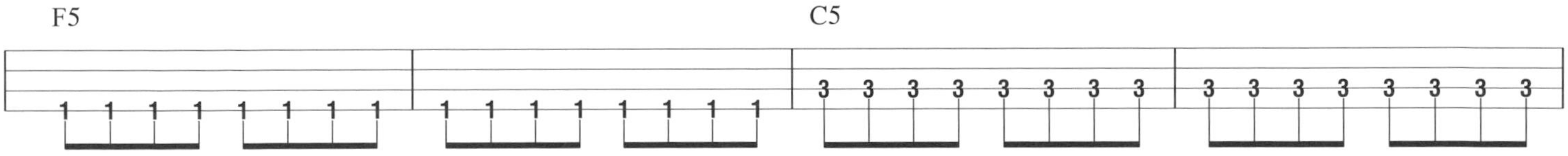
F5
C5

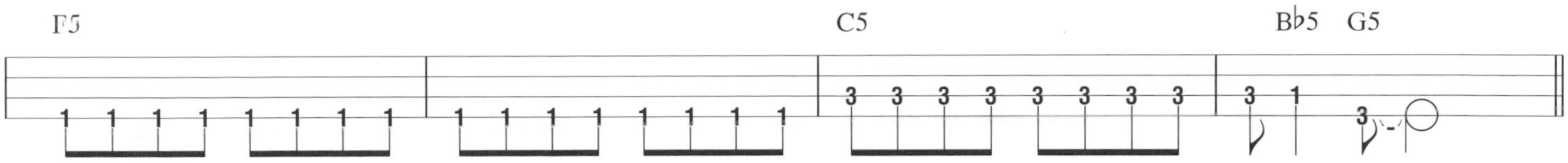
F5
C5
B♭5 G5

Interlude

D.S. al Coda

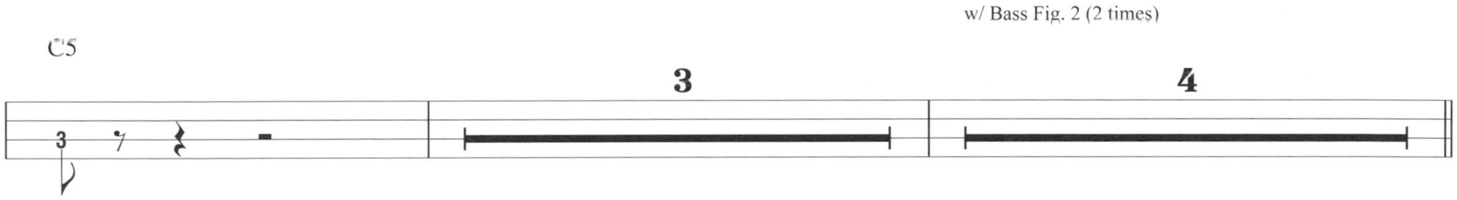
w/ Bass Fig. 2 (2 times)
C5
3
4

Coda

Outro-Guitar Solo

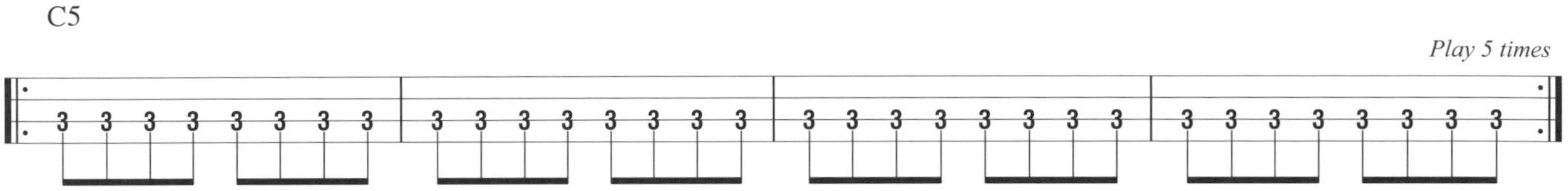
C5
Play 5 times

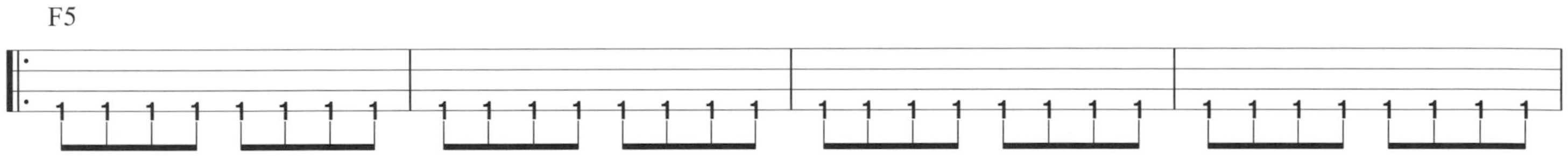
F5

Repeat and fade

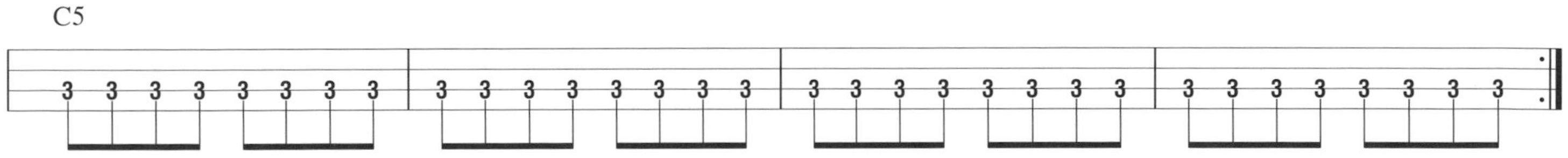
C5

Additional Lyrics

2. Gold watch, diamond ring,
I ain't missin' not a single thing.
Cuff links, stick pin,
When I step out I'm gonna do you in.

3. Top coat, top hat,
An' I don't worry 'cause my wallet's fat.
Black shades, white gloves,
Lookin' sharp, lookin' for love.

Shut Up and Dance

Words and Music by Ryan McMahon, Ben Berger, Sean Waugaman,
Eli Maiman, Nicholas Petricca and Kevin Ray

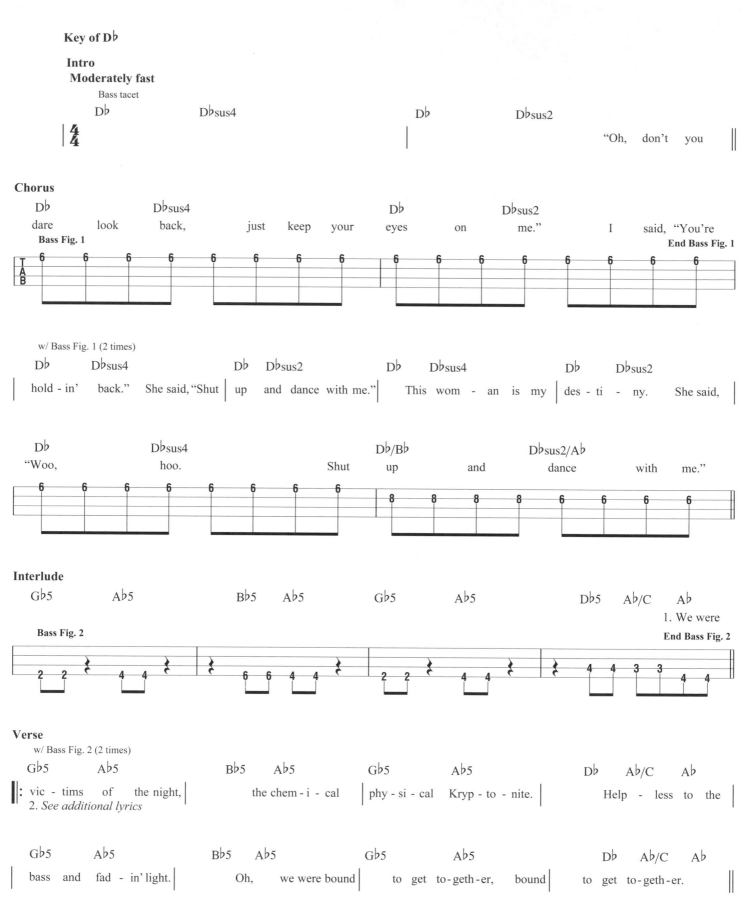

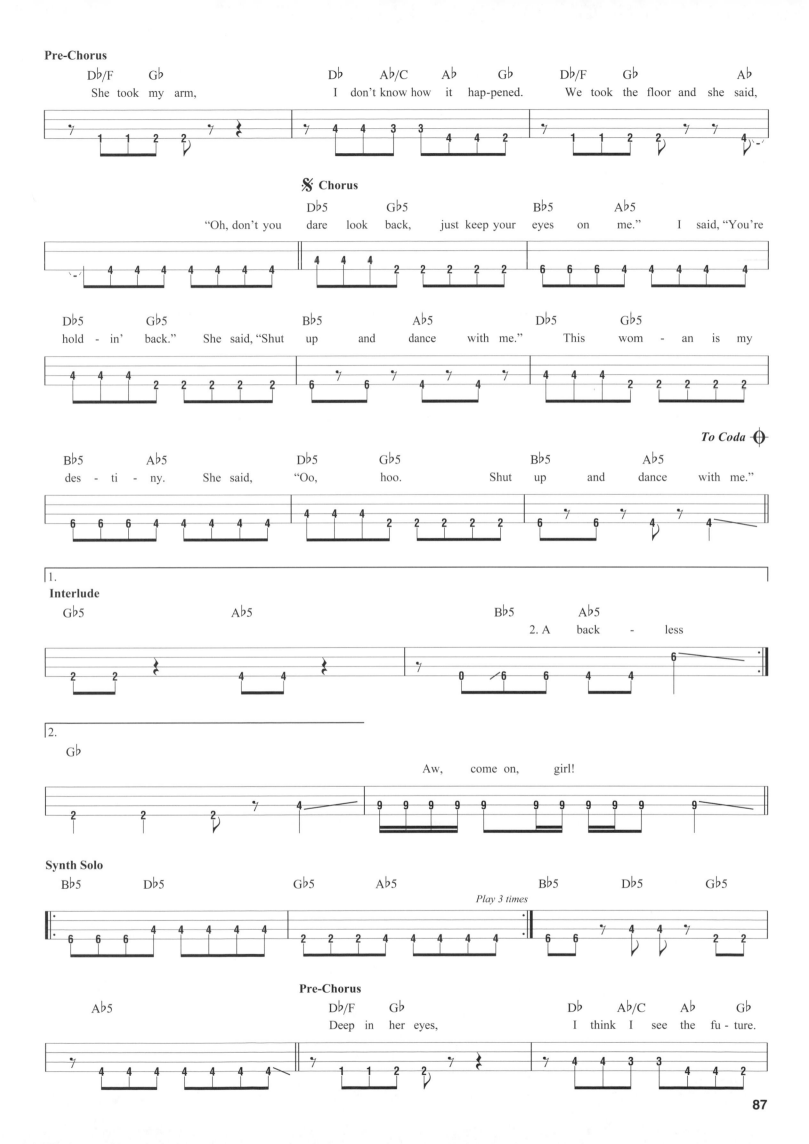

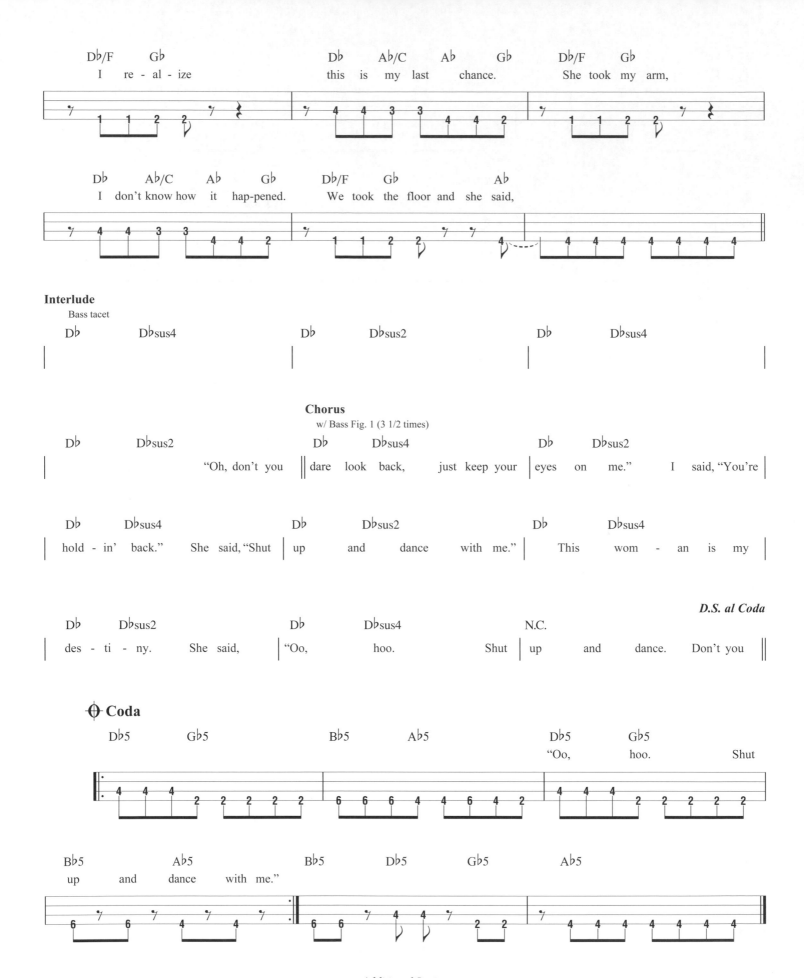

Interlude

Chorus

Coda

D.S. al Coda

Additional Lyrics

2. A backless dress and some beat-up sneaks,
My discotech Juliette teenage dream.
I felt it in my chest as she looked at me.
I knew we were bound to be together,
Bound to be together.

Sunshine of Your Love

Words and Music by Eric Clapton, Jack Bruce and Pete Brown

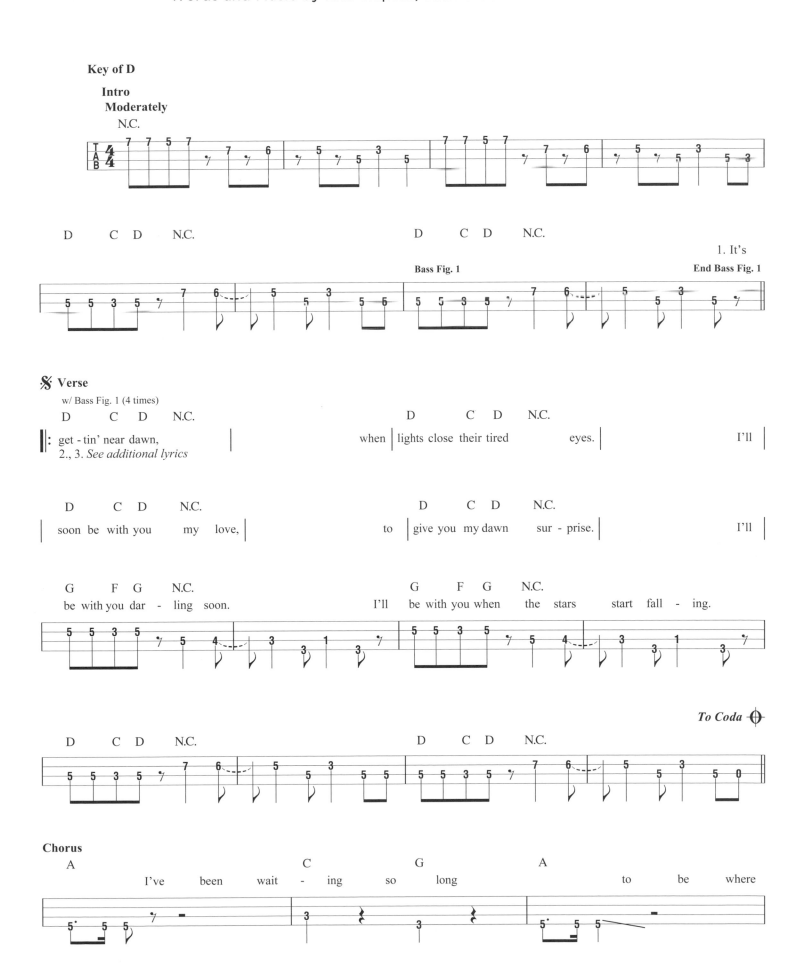

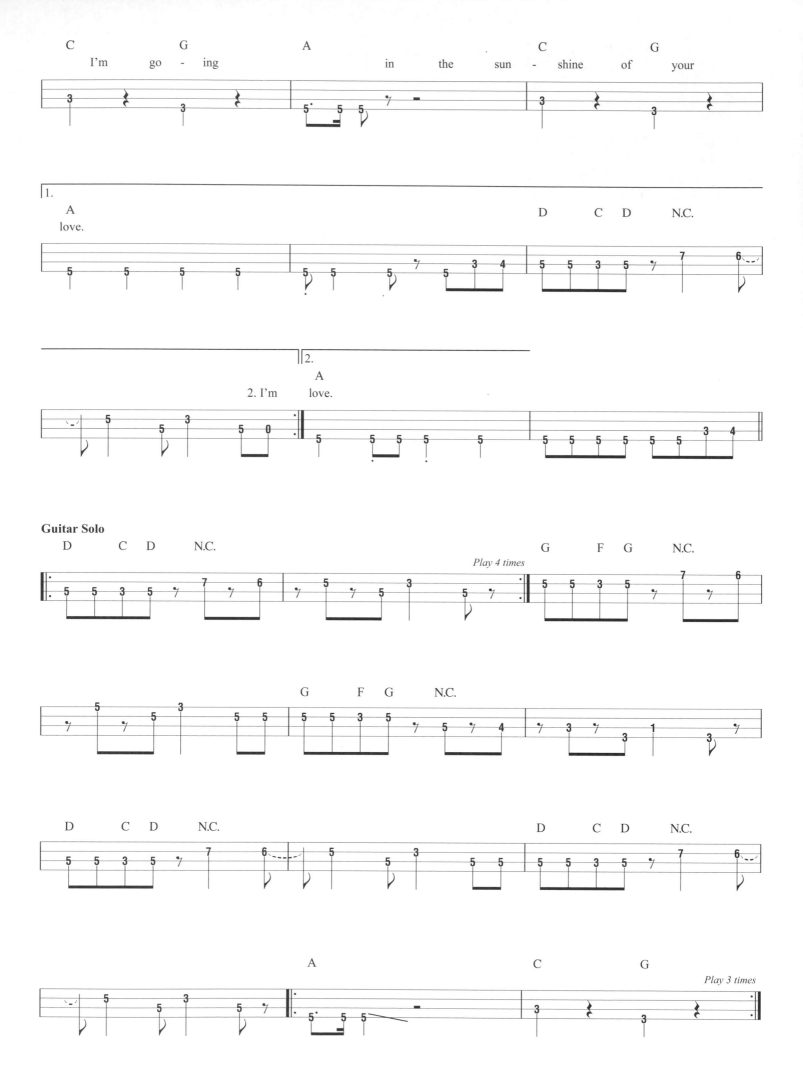

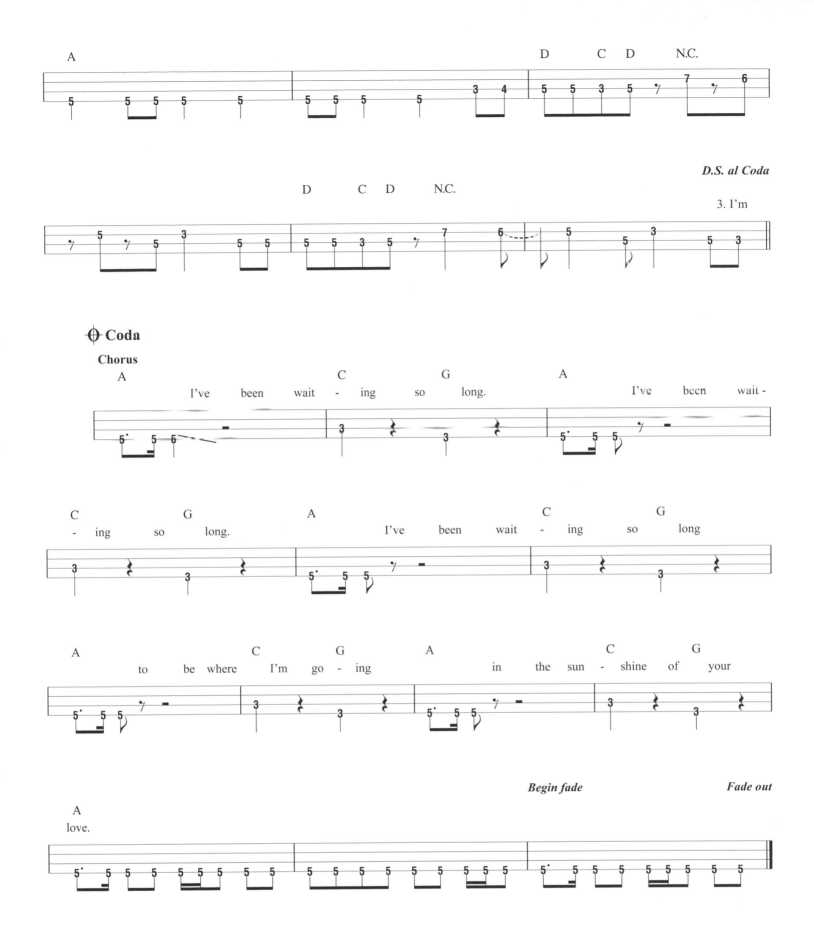

Smells Like Teen Spirit

Words and Music by Kurt Cobain, Krist Novoselic and Dave Grohl

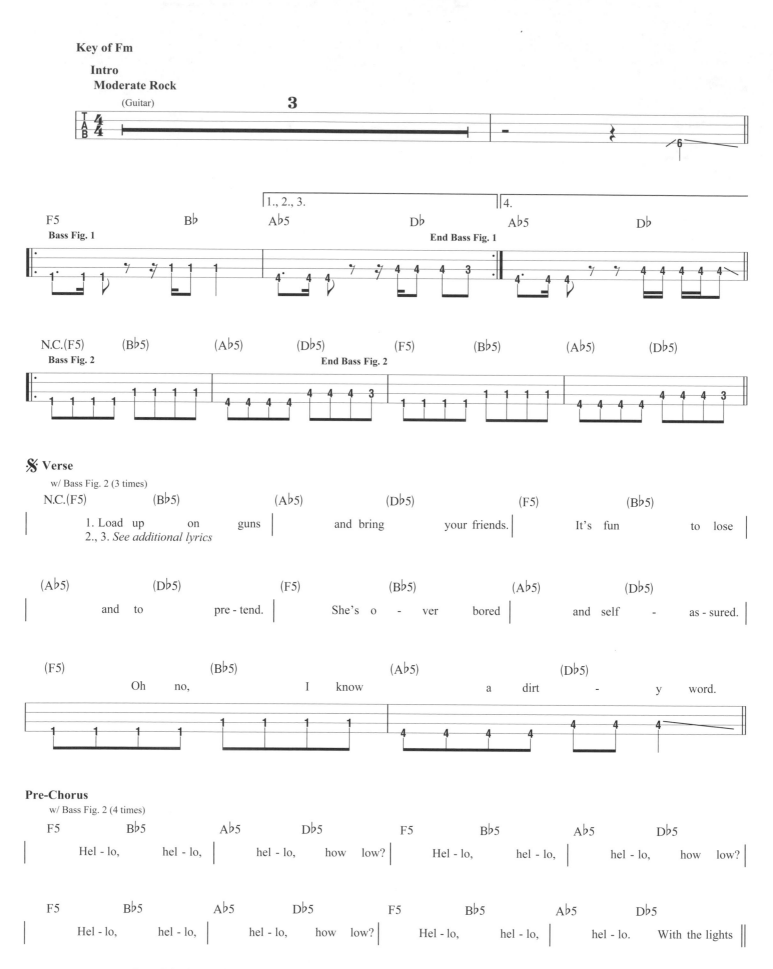

Chorus
w/ Bass Fig. 1 (6 times)

F5	Bb	Ab5	Db	F5	Bb	Ab5	Db
out	it's less dan	- g'rous.	Here we are	now,	en - ter - tain	us.	I feel stu -

F5	Bb	Ab5	Db	F5	Bb	Ab5	Db
- pid	and con - ta	- gious.	Here we are	now,	en - ter - tain	us.	A mu - lat -

To Coda ⊕

F5	Bb	Ab5	Db	F5	Bb	Ab5	Db
- to,	an al - bi	- no,	a mos - qui	- to,	my li - bi	- do.	Yay,

Bridge
F5 E5 F5 Gb5 N.C. F5/C E5/C F5/C Bb5 Ab5 G5 F5 E5 F5 Gb5 N.C. F5/C E5/C F5/C Bb5 Ab5 G5

yay,   yay.

Guitar Solo
w/ Bass Fig. 1 (8 times)

16

D.S. al Coda

w/ Bass Fig. 2 (2 times)

4

⊕ Coda

Outro
w/ Bass Fig. 1 (4 times)

	F5		Bb	Ab5	Db	F5	Bb
	- to,		my li - bi	- do,	a de - ni	‖: - al,	a de - ni -

Ab5	Db	F5	Bb	Ab5	Db
- al,	a de - ni	- al,	a de - ni	- al,	a de - ni - :‖

Freely
F5

- al!

Additional Lyrics

2. I'm worse at what I do best,
And for this gift I feel blessed.
Our little group has always been
And always will until the end.

3. And I forget just why I taste.
Oo, yeah, I guess it makes you smile,
I found it hard, it's hard to find.
Oh well, whatever, never mind.

Stand by Me

Words and Music by Jerry Leiber, Mike Stoller and Ben E. King

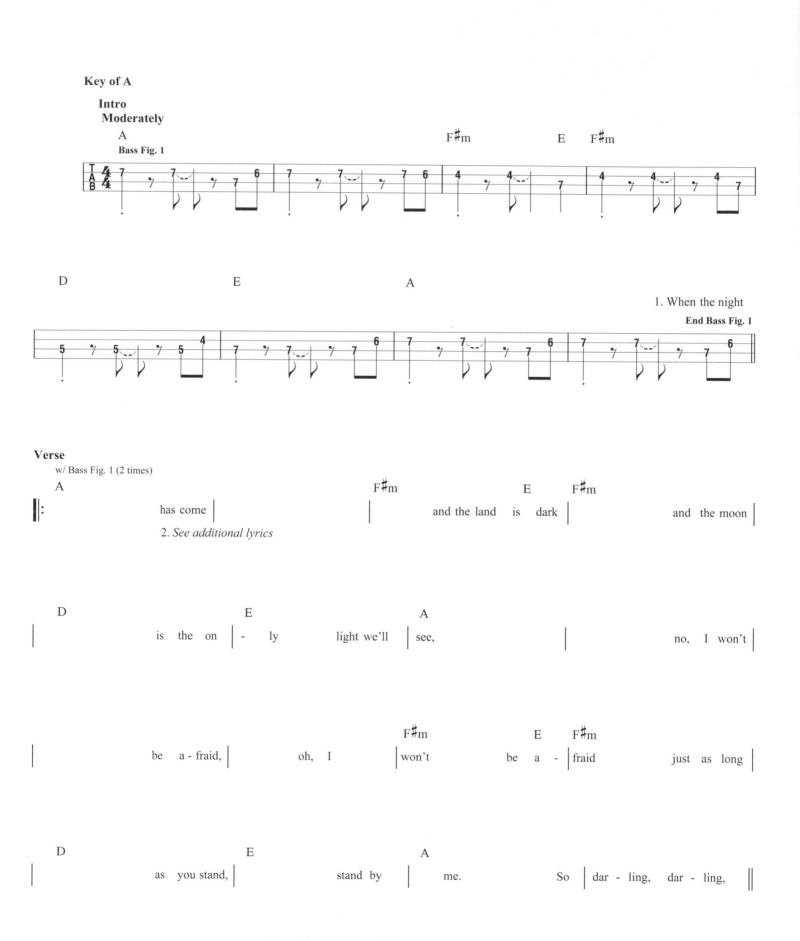

Chorus
w/ Bass Fig. 1

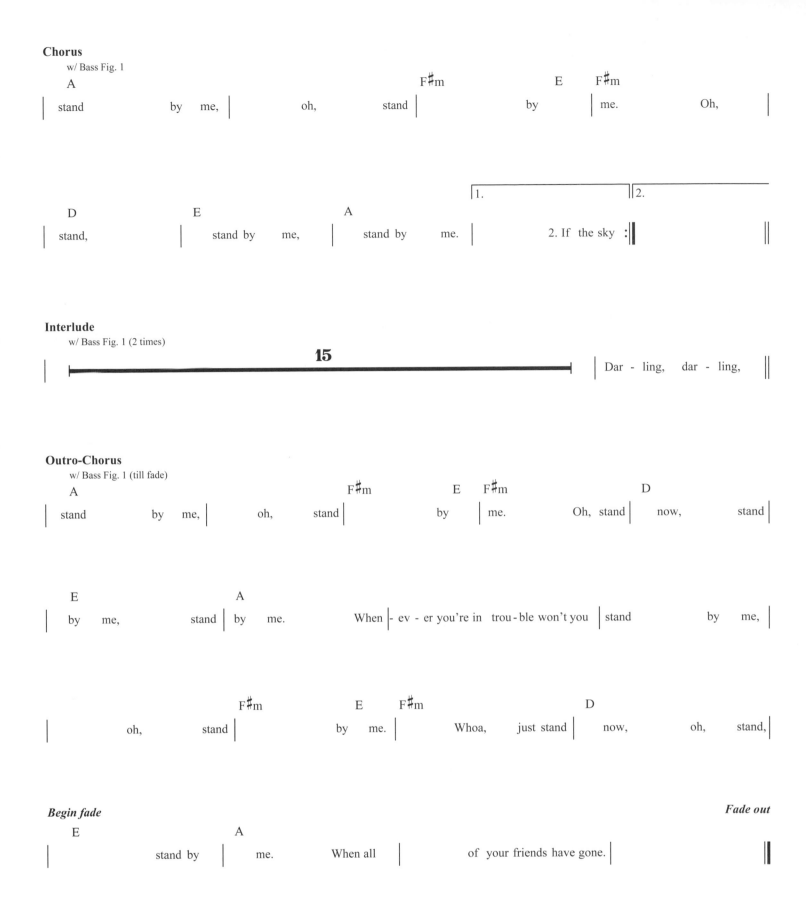

A				F#m		E	F#m		
stand		by	me,	oh,	stand		by	me.	Oh,

	1.		2.	
D		E		A
stand,		stand by	me,	stand by	me.	2. If the sky	

Interlude
w/ Bass Fig. 1 (2 times)

15

Dar - ling, dar - ling,

Outro-Chorus
w/ Bass Fig. 1 (till fade)

A				F#m		E	F#m		D	
stand		by	me,	oh,	stand		by	me.	Oh, stand	now,	stand

E			A						
by	me,	stand	by	me.	When ev - er you're in trou - ble won't you	stand		by	me,

		F#m		E	F#m		D	
oh,	stand		by	me.	Whoa,	just stand	now,	oh,	stand,

Begin fade   *Fade out*

E			A					
	stand by		me.	When all		of your friends have gone.	

Additional Lyrics

2. If the sky that we look upon should tumble and fall,
Or the mountains should crumble to the sea,
I won't cry, I won't cry. No, I won't shed a tear,
Just as long as you stand, stand by me.
And darlin', darlin'...

Sweet Home Alabama

Words and Music by Ronnie Van Zant, Ed King and Gary Rossington

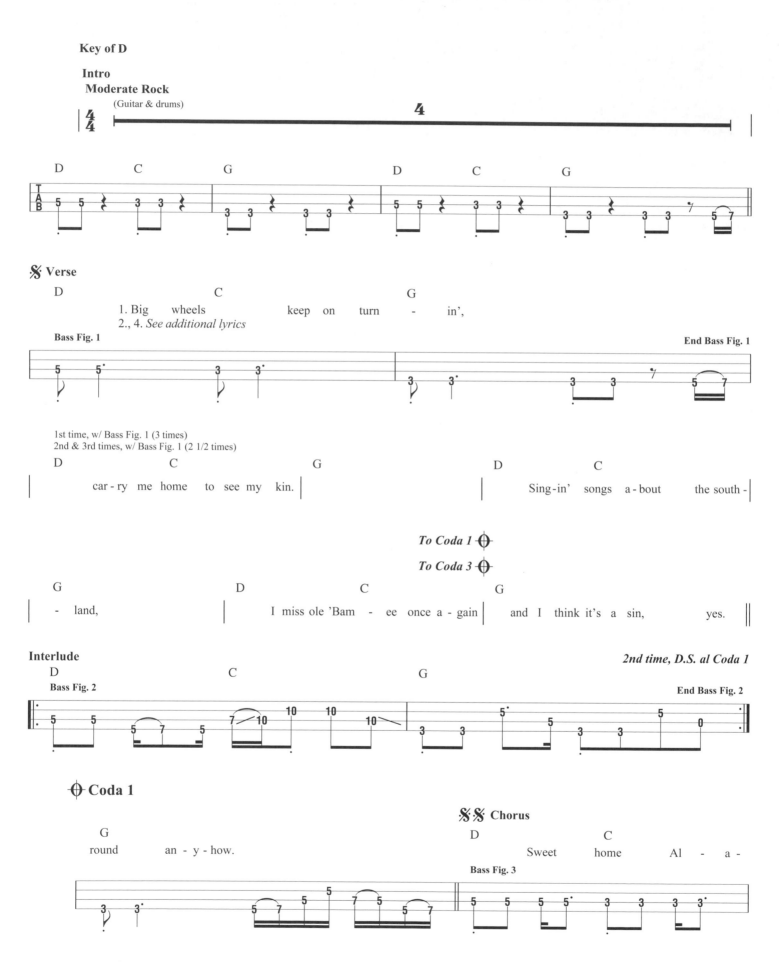

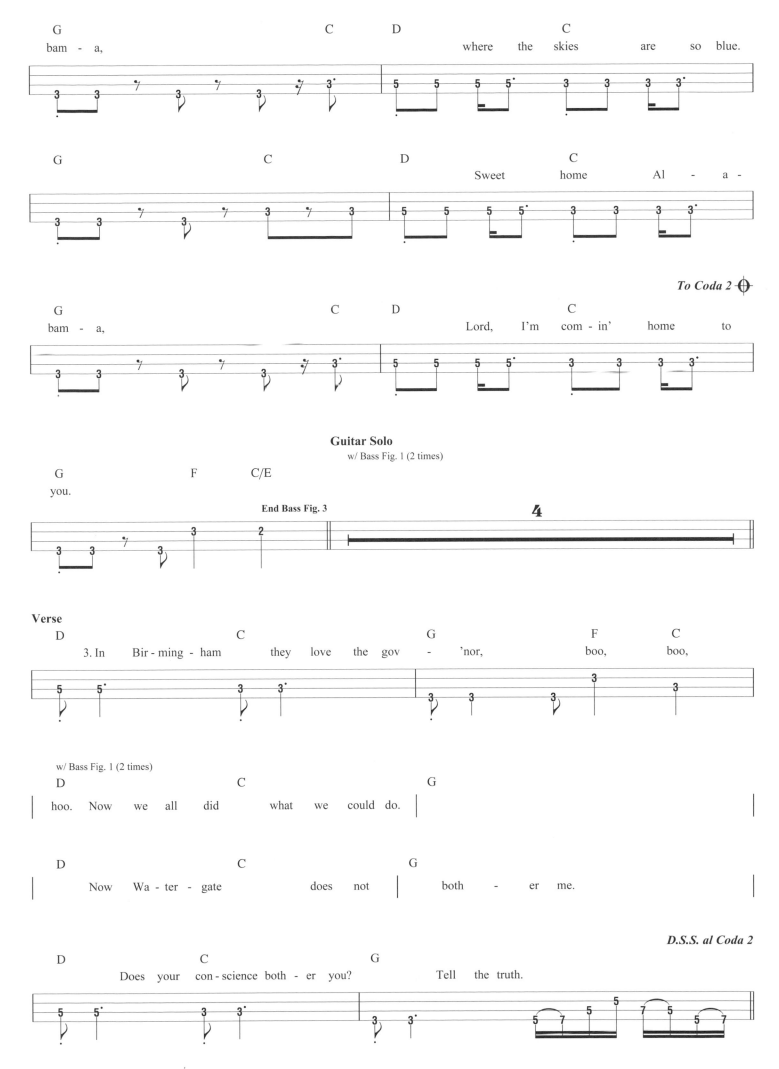

To Coda 2

Guitar Solo
w/ Bass Fig. 1 (2 times)

End Bass Fig. 3

Verse

D.S.S. al Coda 2

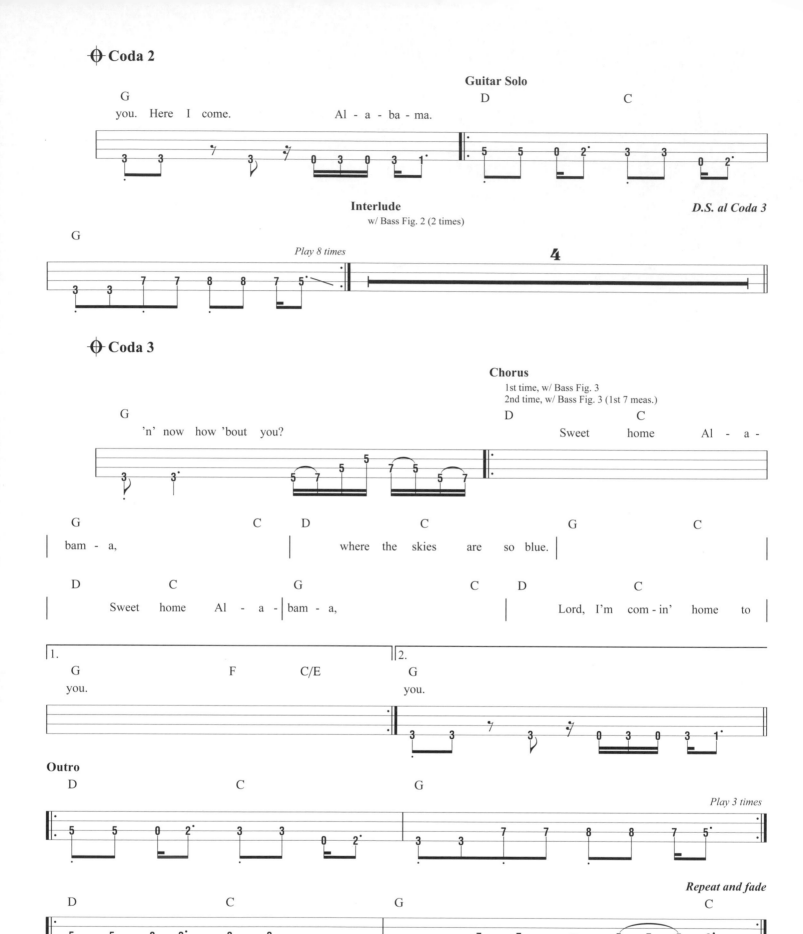

Additional Lyrics

2. Well, I heard Mister Young sing about her.
Well, I heard old Neil put 'er down.
Well, I hope Neil Young will remember,
A southern man don't need him around anyhow.

4. Now Muscle Shoals has got the Swampers,
An' they been known to pick a song or two.
Lord, they get me off so much.
They pick me up when I'm feelin' blue, 'n' now how 'bout you?

Sweet Home Chicago

Words and Music by Robert Johnson

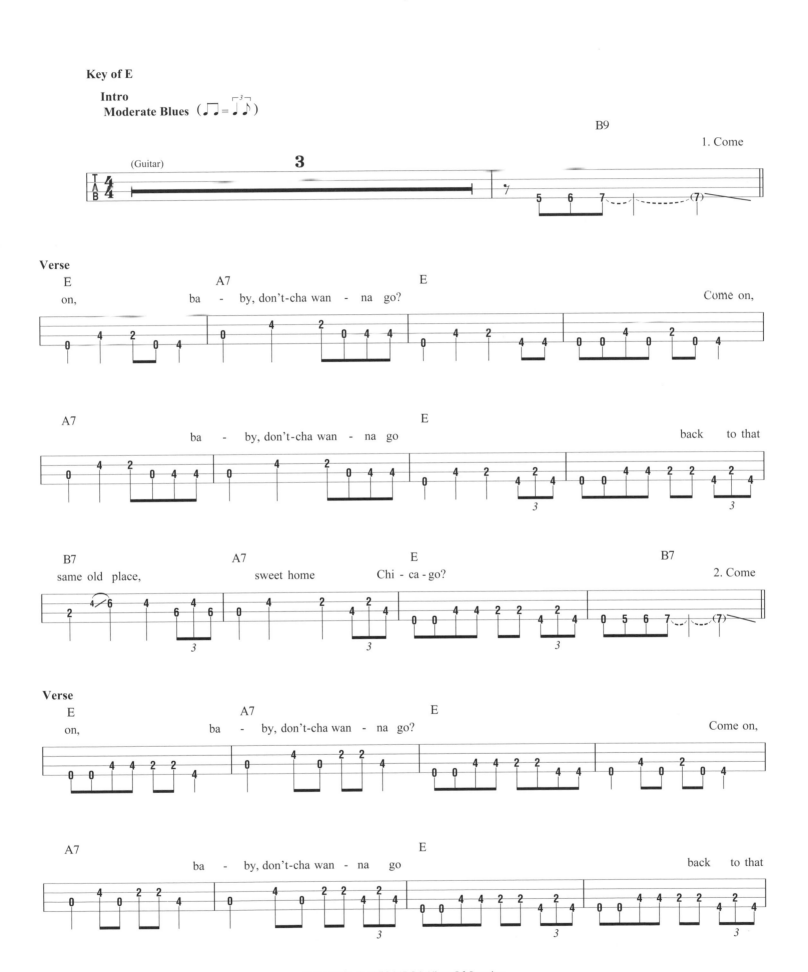

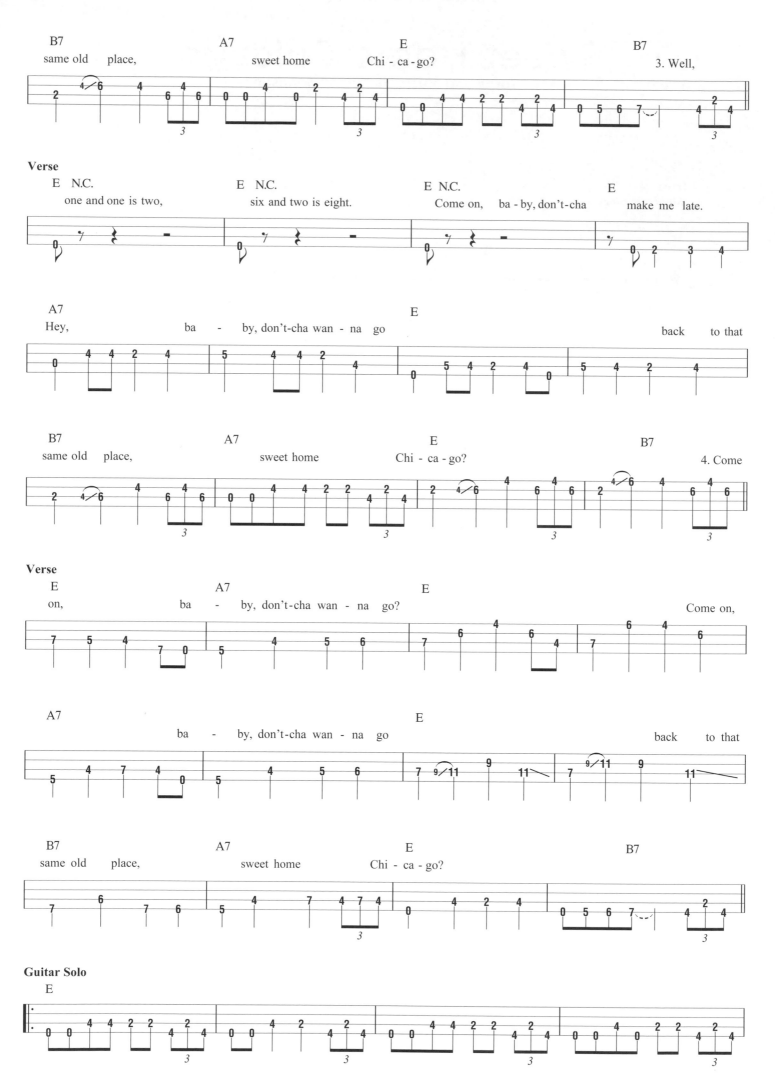

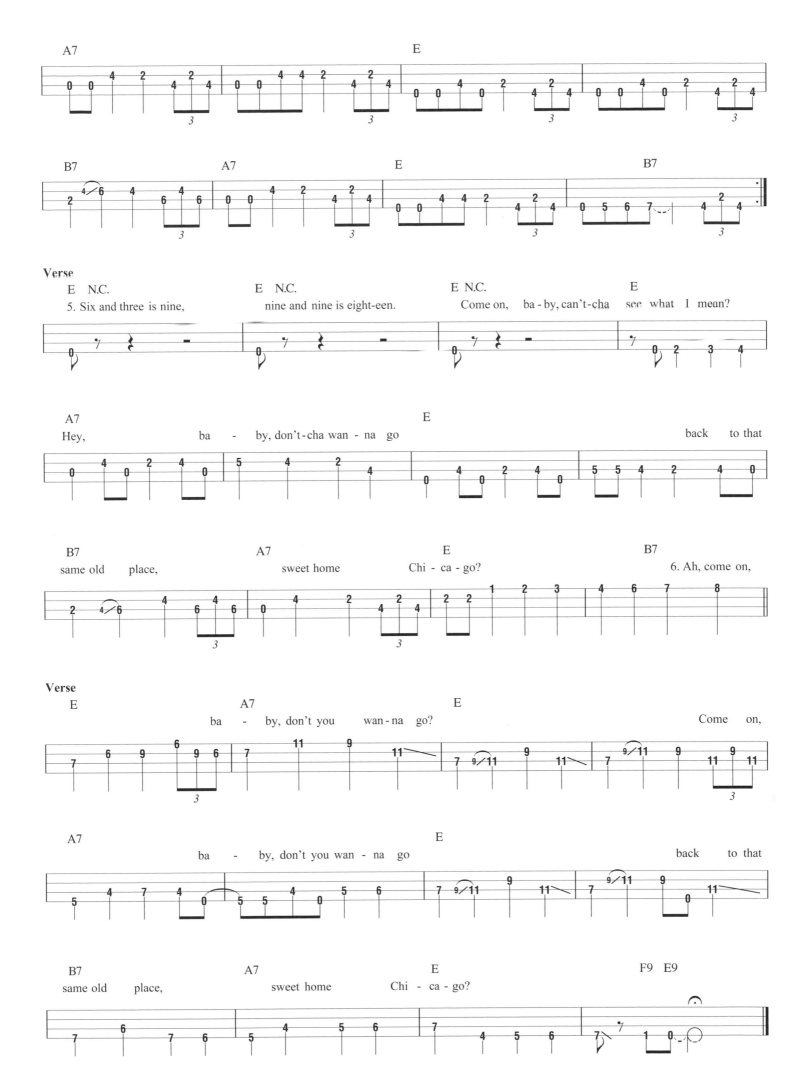

Thinking Out Loud

Words and Music by Ed Sheeran and Amy Wadge

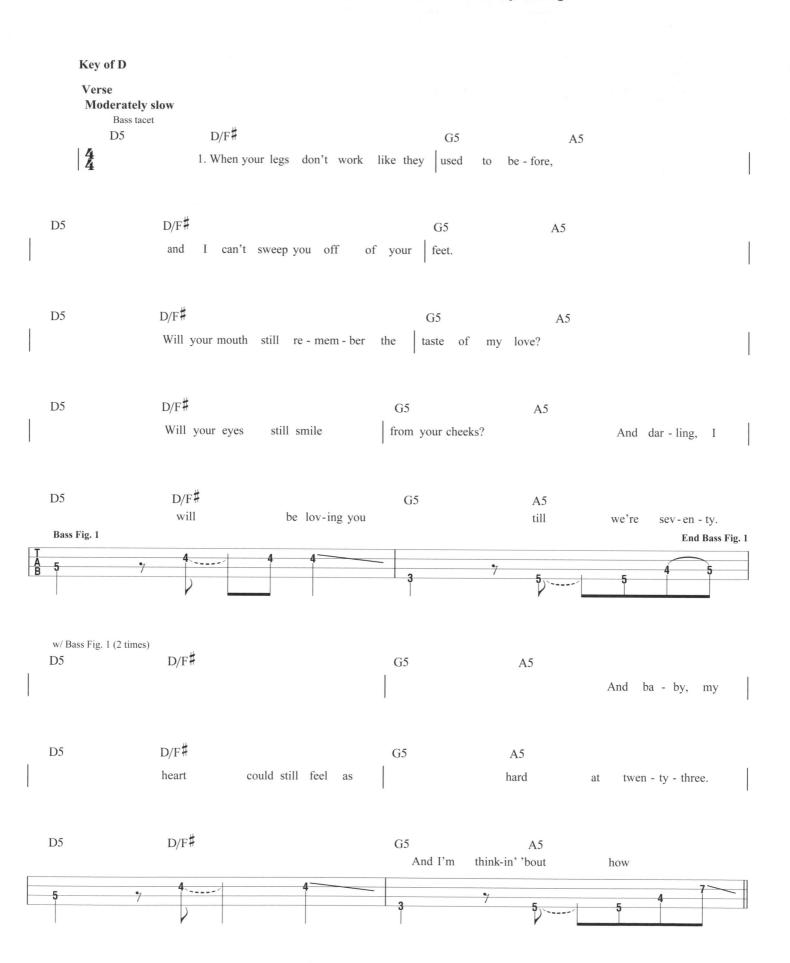

Verse

w/ Bass Fig. 2 (8 times)

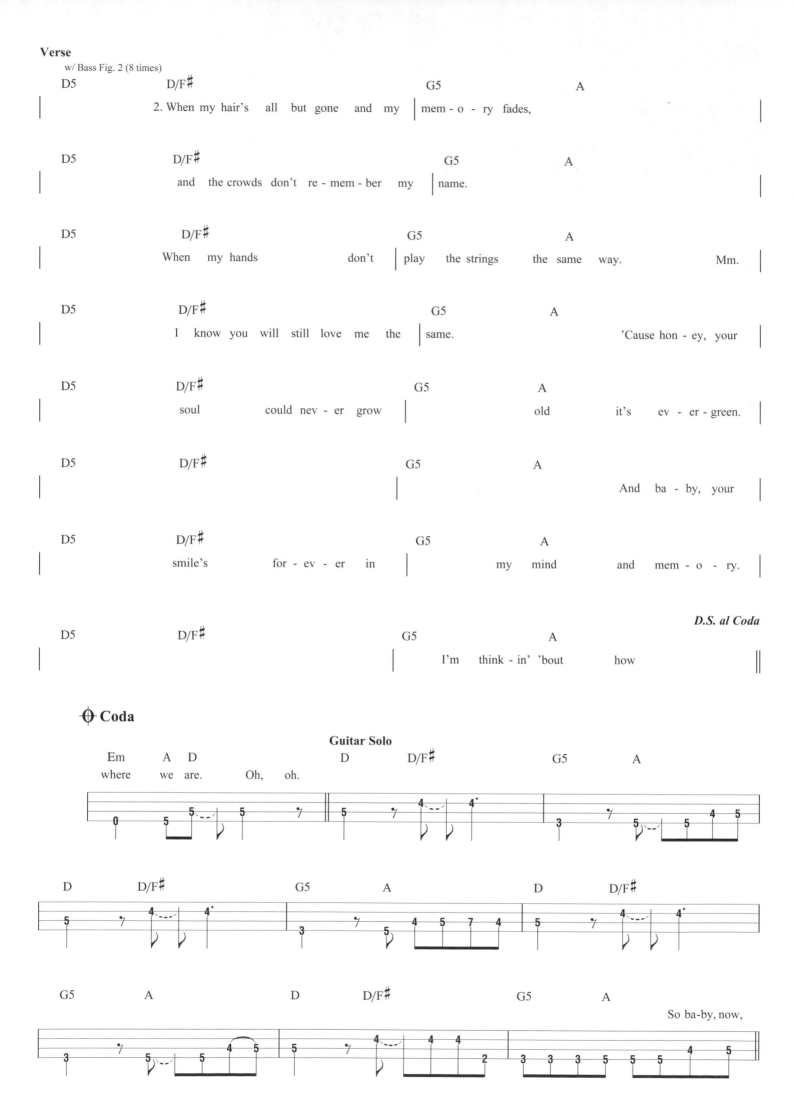

D5   D/F♯   G5   A

2. When my hair's all but gone and my mem - o - ry fades,

D5   D/F♯   G5   A

and the crowds don't re - mem - ber my name.

D5   D/F♯   G5   A

When my hands don't play the strings the same way. Mm.

D5   D/F♯   G5   A

I know you will still love me the same. 'Cause hon - ey, your

D5   D/F♯   G5   A

soul could nev - er grow old it's ev - er - green.

D5   D/F♯   G5   A

And ba - by, your

D5   D/F♯   G5   A

smile's for - ev - er in my mind and mem - o - ry.

D.S. al Coda

D5   D/F♯   G5   A

I'm think - in' 'bout how

⊕ Coda

Guitar Solo

Em   A   D   D   D/F♯   G5   A

where we are. Oh, oh.

D   D/F♯   G5   A   D   D/F♯

G5   A   D   D/F♯   G5   A

So ba - by, now,

Chorus

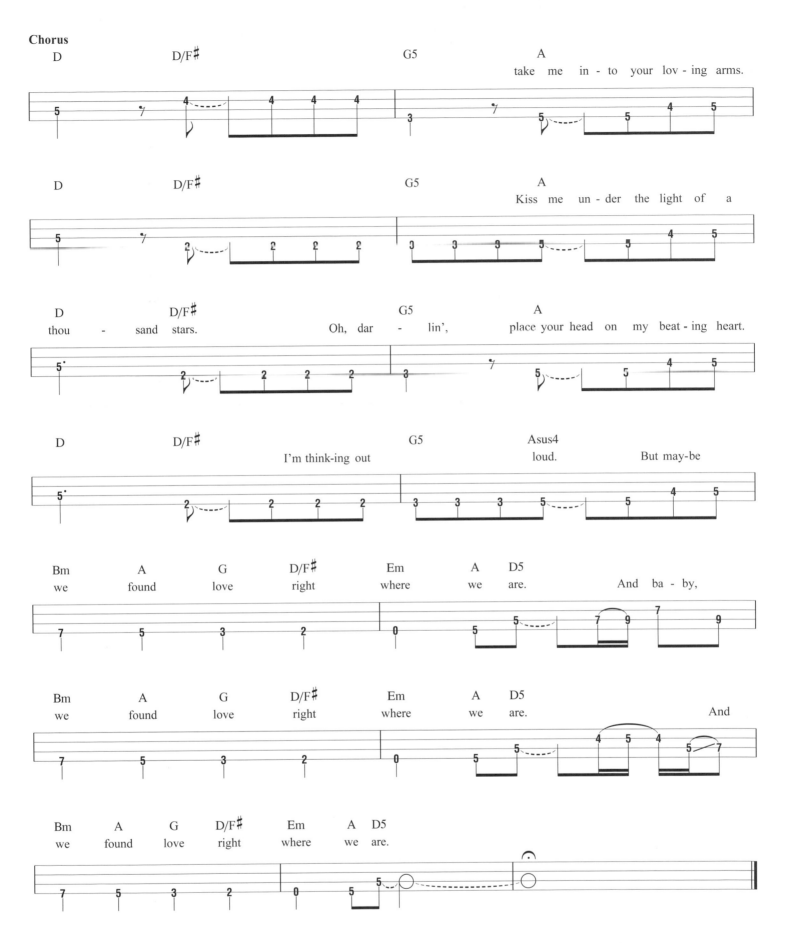

Additional Lyrics

Pre-Chorus I'm thinkin' 'bout how people fall in love in mysterious ways
And maybe it's all part of a plan.
Well, I'll just keep on making the same mistakes;
Hoping that you'll understand.
That baby, now...

Three Little Birds

Words and Music by Bob Marley

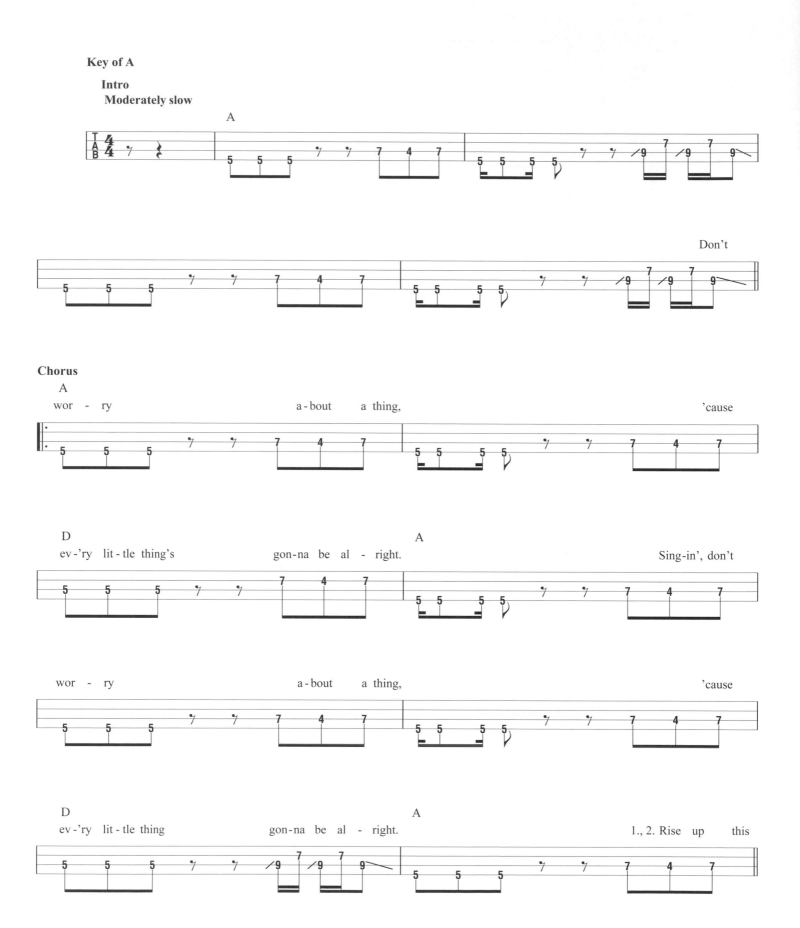

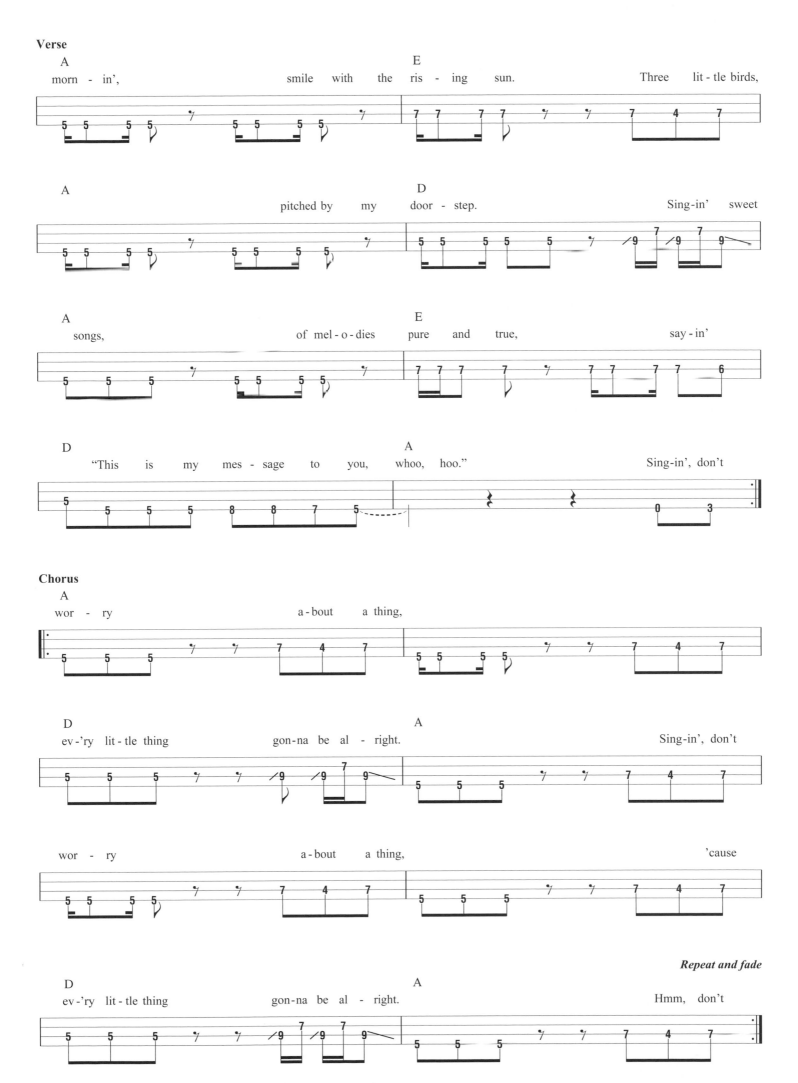

25 or 6 to 4

Words and Music by Robert Lamm

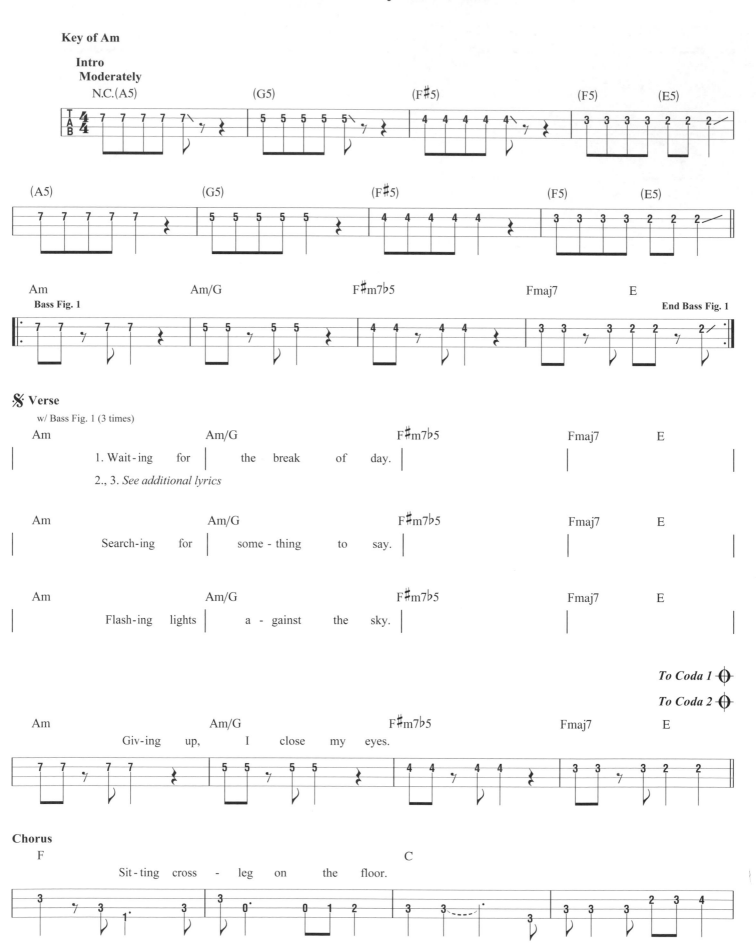

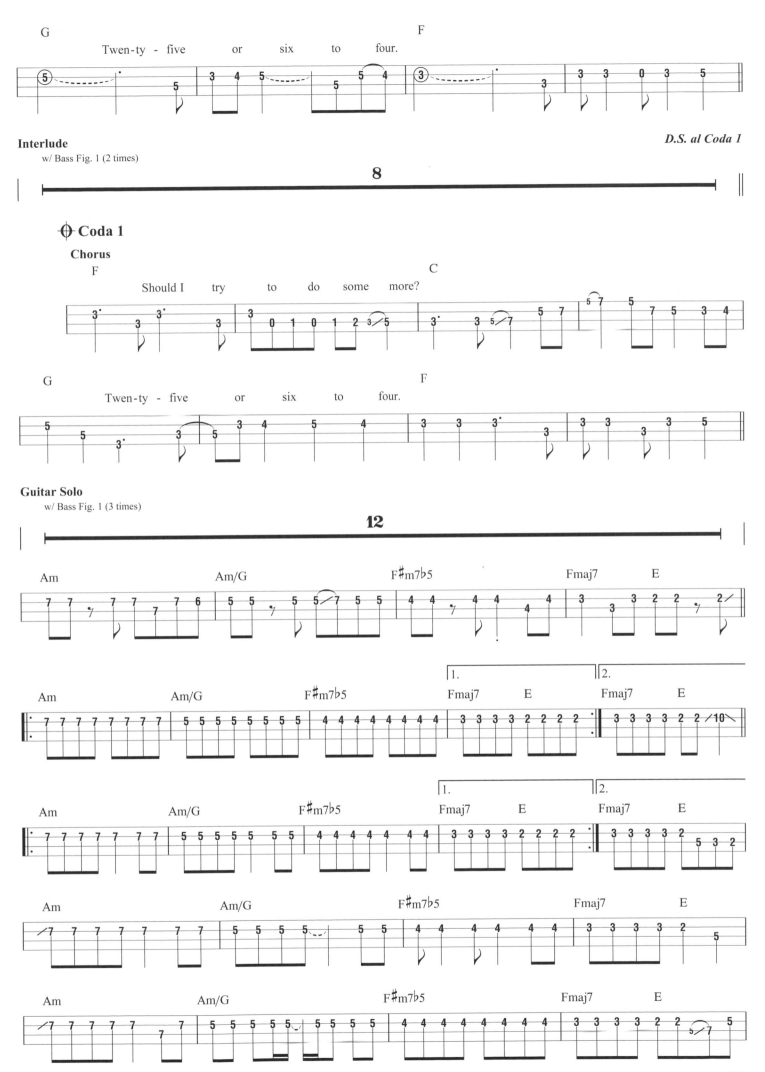

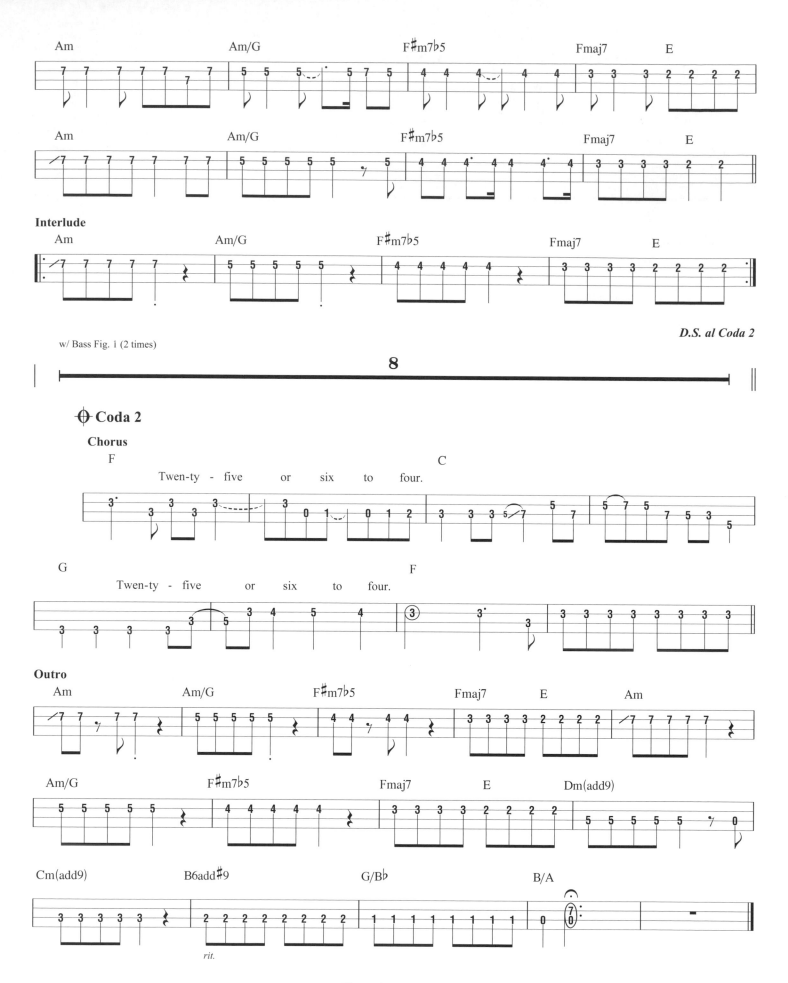

D.S. al Coda 2

w/ Bass Fig. 1 (2 times)

Coda 2

Chorus

Twen-ty - five   or   six   to   four.

Twen-ty - five   or   six   to   four.

Outro

rit.

Additional Lyrics

2. Staring blindly into space.
   Getting up to splash my face.
   Wanting just to stay awake.
   Wond'ring how much I can take.

3. Feeling like I ought to sleep.
   Spinning room is sinking deep.
   Searching for something to say.
   Waiting for the break of day.

Wake Me Up When September Ends

Words by Billie Joe
Music by Green Day

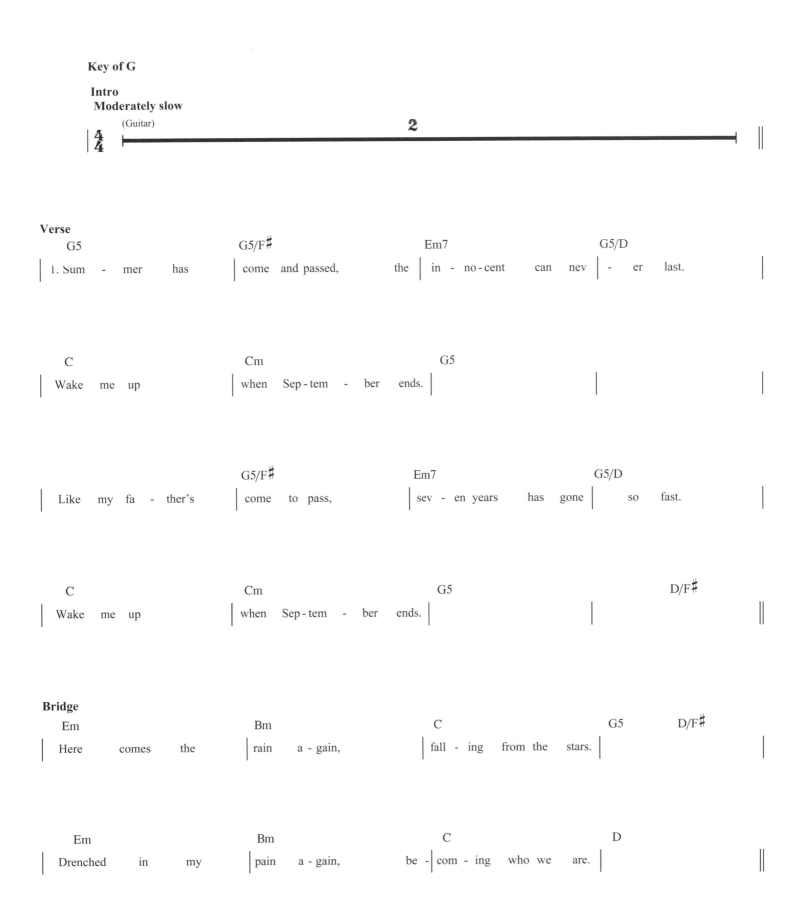

Key of G

Intro
Moderately slow
(Guitar)
4/4 | — 2 — ||

Verse

G5 · · · · · · · · · G5/F♯ · · · · · · · Em7 · · · · · · · · G5/D
| 1. Sum - mer has | come and passed, the | in - no - cent can nev | - er last. |

C · · · · · · · · · · · Cm · · · · · · · · · · · G5
| Wake me up | when Sep - tem - ber ends. | | |

· · · · · · · · · · · · G5/F♯ · · · · · · · Em7 · · · · · · · · · G5/D
| Like my fa - ther's | come to pass, | sev - en years has gone | so fast. |

C · · · · · · · · · · · Cm · · · · · · · · · · · G5 · · · · · · · · · · D/F♯
| Wake me up | when Sep - tem - ber ends. | | ||

Bridge

Em · · · · · · · · · · · Bm · · · · · · · · · · · C · · · · · · · · · · G5 · · · · D/F♯
| Here comes the | rain a - gain, | fall - ing from the stars. | |

Em · · · · · · · · · · · Bm · · · · · · · · · · · C · · · · · · · · · · D
| Drenched in my | pain a - gain, | be - com - ing who we are. | ||

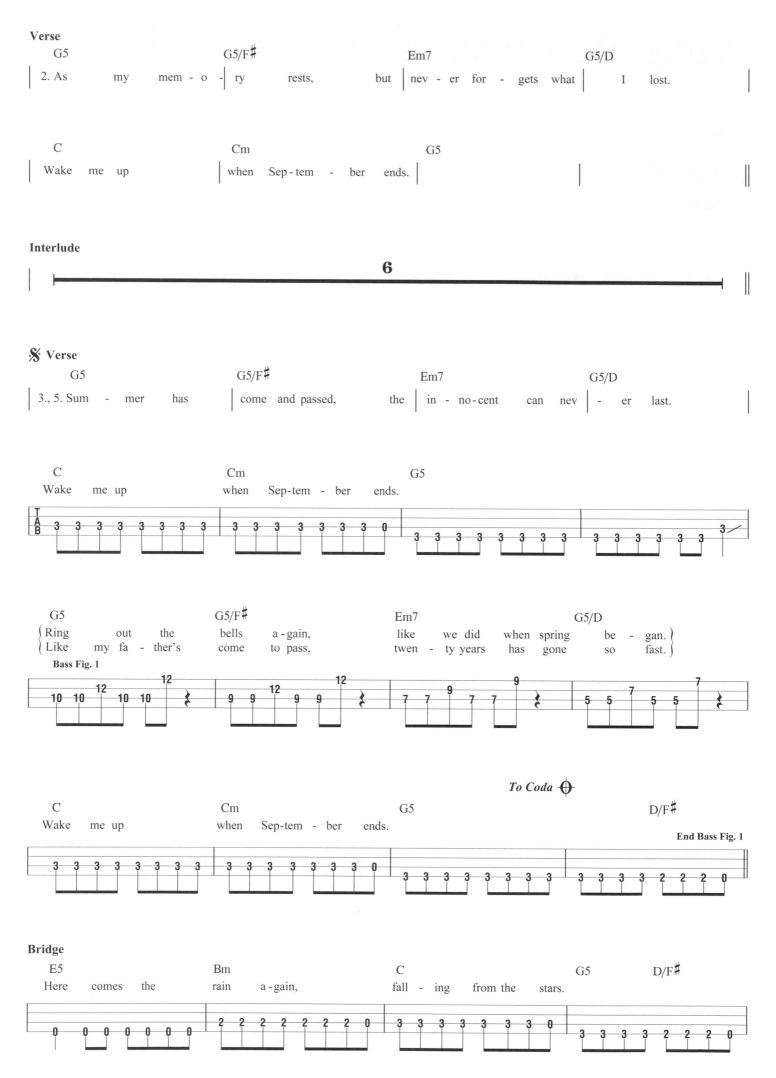

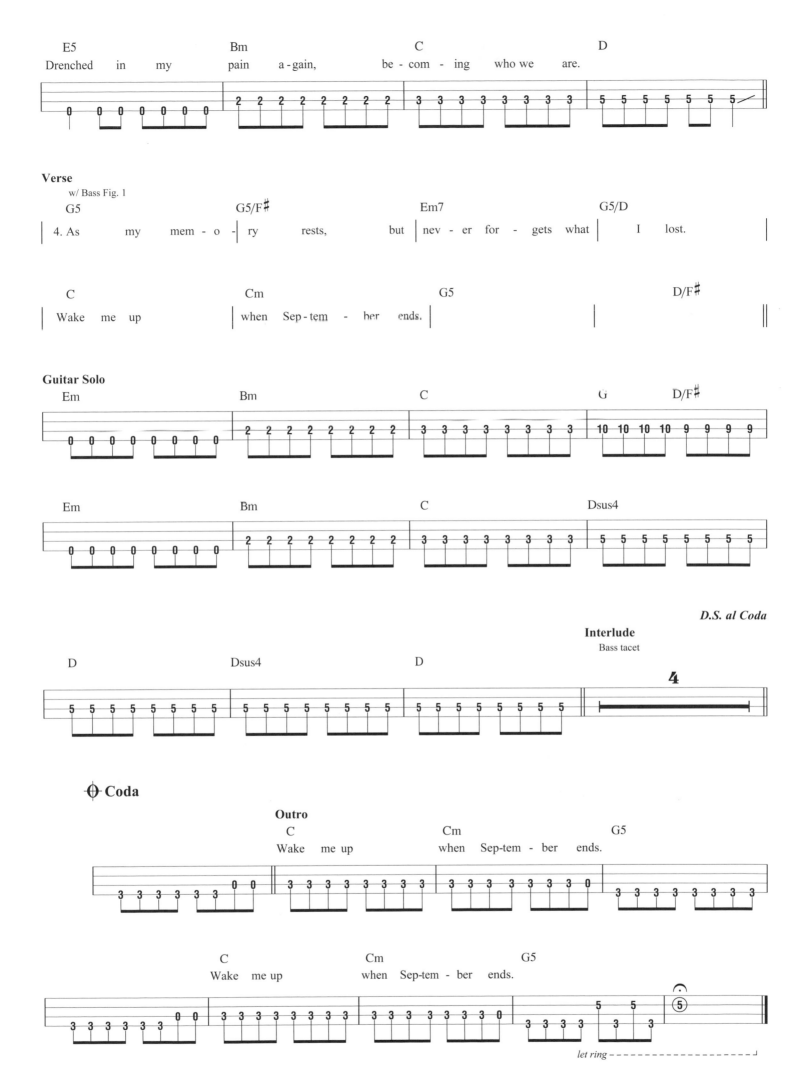

What's Up

Words and Music by Linda Perry

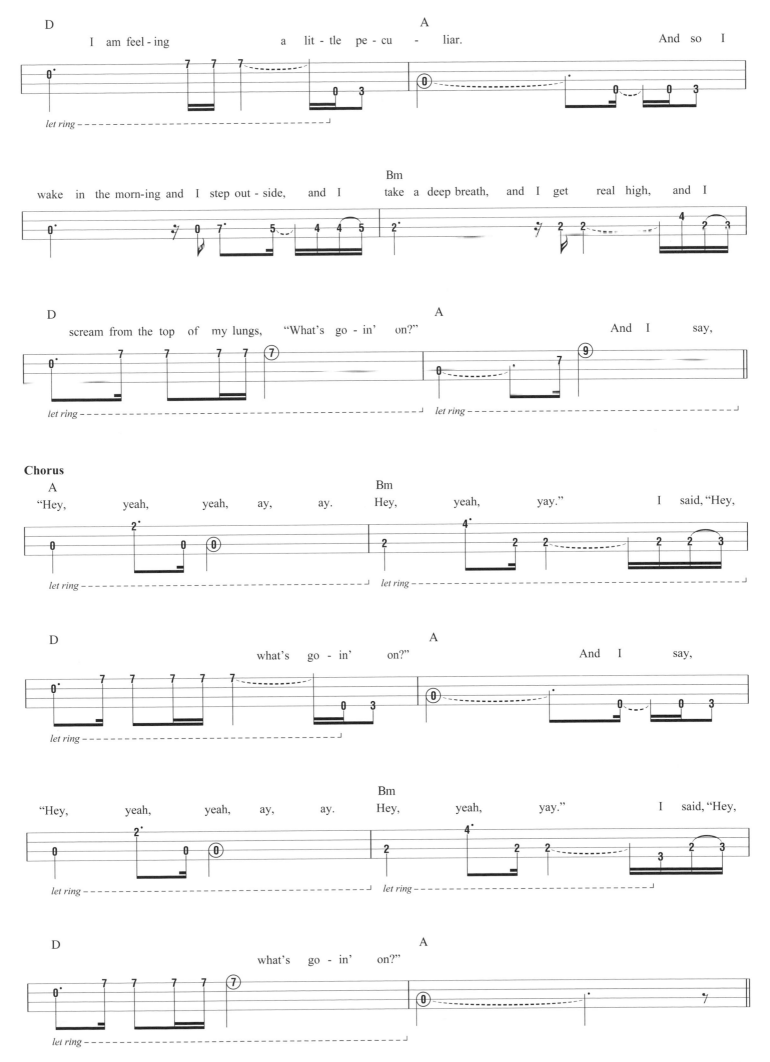

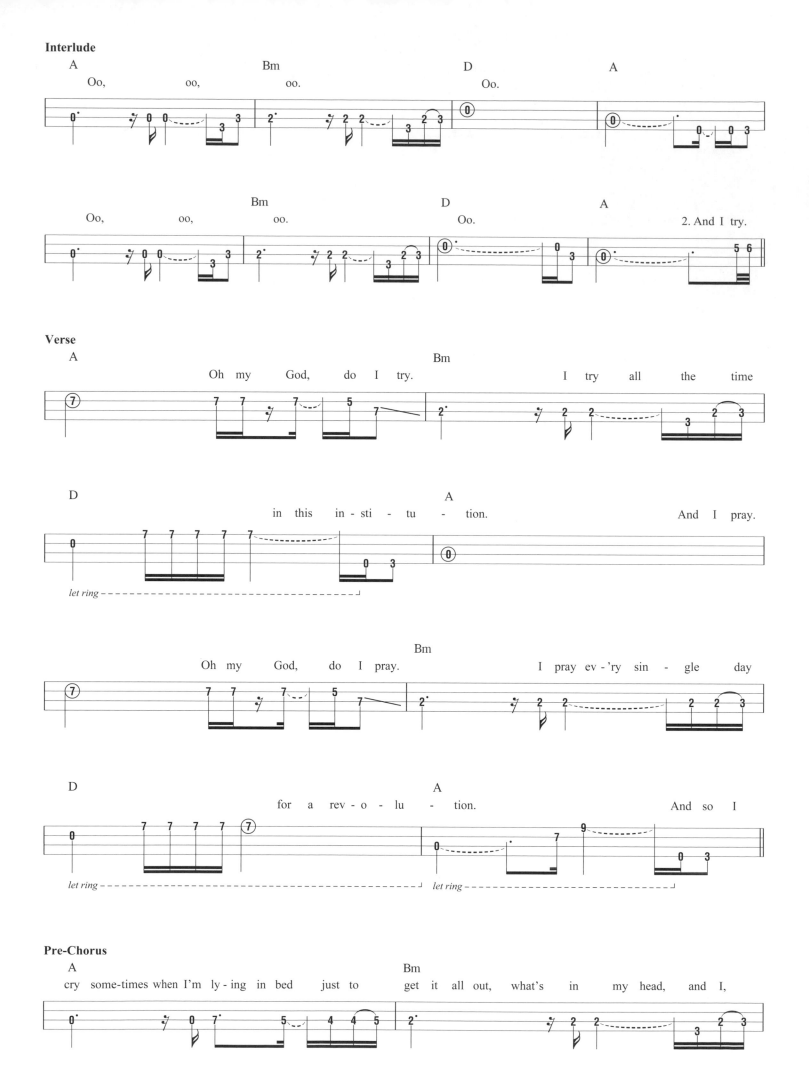

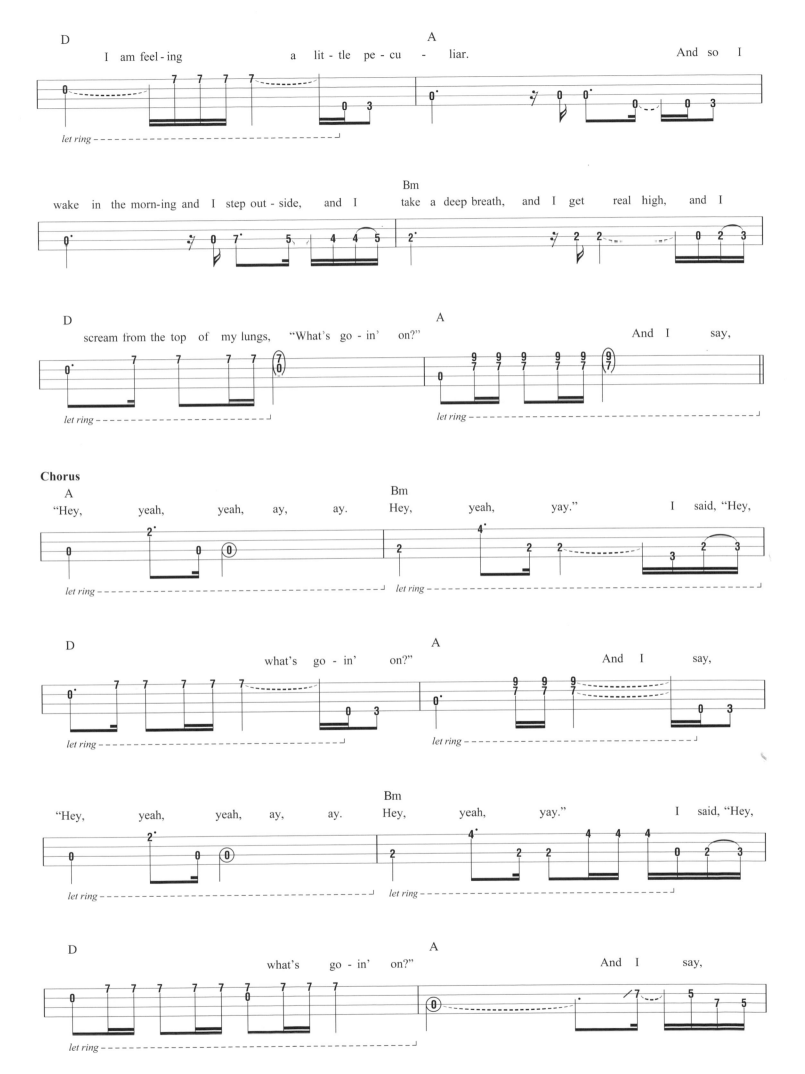

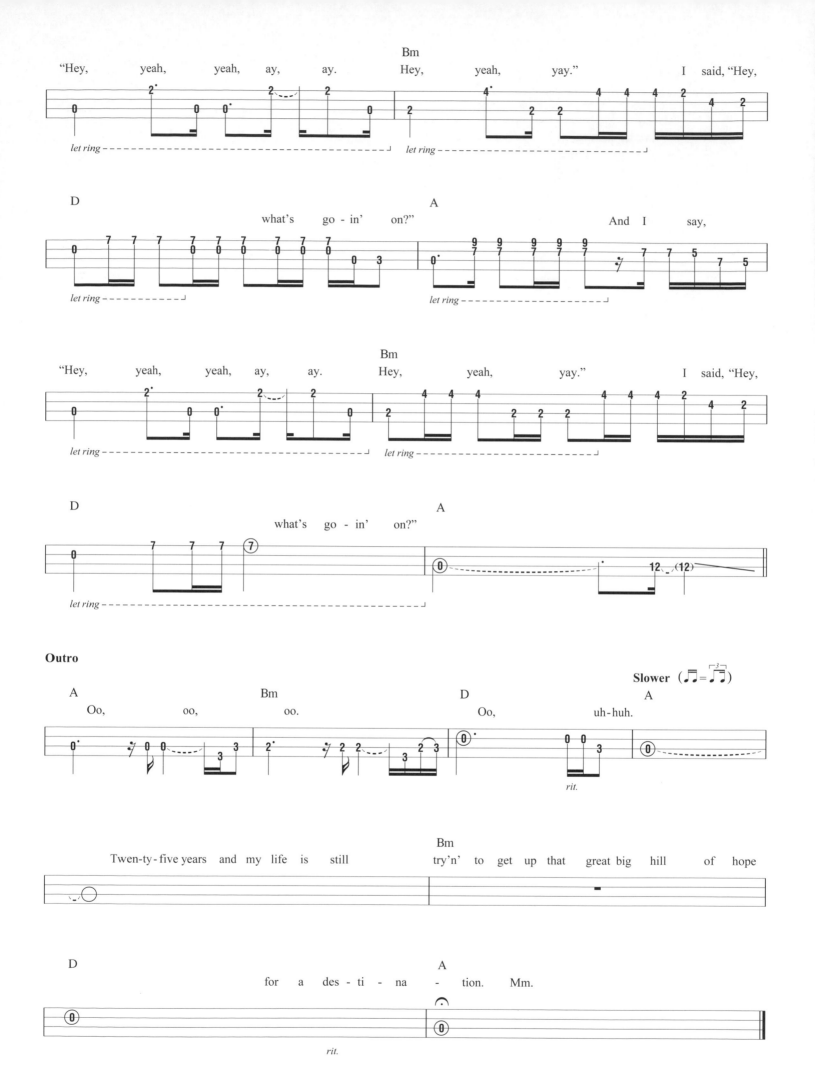